HOW TO MAKE
CERAMICS

by Gertrude Engel

HOW TO Make and Pour Molds
HOW TO Decorate Greenware
HOW TO Apply Glazes
HOW TO Airbrush
HOW TO Use the Potter's Wheel
HOW TO Sculpt Large Figures

OUTSTANDING PROJECTS YOU CAN MAKE:
Bowls • Candlesticks • Tiles
• Harlequin • Figures • Trays

Paragon Assures Easier, Better, More Economical Firing

America's Leading Hobby Kiln

There are many reasons why Paragon leads all others in sales—quality, dependability and performance to name a few. Quantity production of uniformly high quality kilns, designed to the most exacting specifications and thoroughly tested before release for sale is your assurance of the most for your money in any price range. For those who want the very best, it's Paragon—the finest kilns made, yet competitively priced from $21.00 up.

It's so economical to own and operate your own Paragon Kiln. Low first cost, low operating cost—less than 25¢ for most hobby models—and the professional touch you get from a Paragon firing can make your hobby extremely profitable!

Series S. The most advanced design ever offered. Years ahead in engineering and materials used. Our finest kilns, yet offered at a lower price than most first line kilns of similar size.

It's easy to use a Paragon Kiln. Complete instruction book given with each kiln, a real help to beginners! If you would like to know more about this fascinating hobby, write us for a free catalog and the name of a qualified studio or teacher near you.

A Series kilns for porcelain open this fascinating field to every hobbyist, regardless of budget. Easy to fire, economical to operate, and very low first cost. Excellent for all other firing.

FULL YEAR FACTORY GUARANTEE ON ALL KILNS

WRITE FOR FREE CATALOG

PARAGON INDUSTRIES, INC.

P. O. Box 10133   •   Dallas 7, Texas

1

Wedgwood photo

how to make
CERAMICS
by Gertrude Engel

A FAWCETT BOOK	•	NUMBER 344
LARRY EISINGER	•	EDITOR-IN-CHIEF
GEORGE TILTON	•	MANAGING EDITOR
HAROLD KELLY	•	ART EDITOR

W. H. Fawcett, Jr. . . . . President

Roger Fawcett . . . . General Manager

Ralph Daigh . . . . Editorial Director

James B. Boynton . . . . Advertising Director

Al Allard . . . . Art Director

Ralph Mattison . . . . Associate Art Director

Annette Packer . . . . Production Director

MILTON SALAMON . . . . **EDITOR**

SILVIO LEMBO . . . . ASSOCIATE ART EDITOR

Nick Carlucci . . . . Assistant Art Editor

Murray Cooper . . . . Art Associate

Harold E. Price . . . . Art Associate

Michael Gaynor . . . . Art Associate

Larry Flanagan . . . . Art Associate

John S. Selvaggio . . . . Art Associate

Phyllis J. Goodman . . . . Production Editor

Nancy Kay . . . . Assistant Production Editor

HOW TO MAKE CERAMICS, Fawcett Book 344, is published by Fawcett Pub-
lications, Inc., Greenwich, Connecticut. Editorial and Advertising Offices:
67 West 44th Street, New York 36, New York. General Offices: Fawcett
Building, Greenwich, Connecticut. Gordon Fawcett—Secretary-Treasurer.
Roscoe Fawcett—Circulation Director. Trademark of Fawcett Publications,
Inc. Printed in U. S. A. Copyright 1957 by Fawcett Publications, Inc.

Cover photos by Simon Nathan,
taken with Heiland Strobonar lighting

CONTENTS

Author's Introduction   4

Ceramics Through the Ages   5

Ceramics as a Hobby 14

How to Start: Your Tools 20

Clays 26

Molds—How to Make Them 31

Casting and Finishing 38

    Drape—Molded Ash Tray 39

    Ash Tray from 1-Piece Mold 42

    Making a Ceramic Dog 44

Hand-Modeling Pottery 48

    Slab Method: Flower Vase 50

    Cutaway Slab: Candlestick 55

    Coil Method: Decorative Bowl 58

Sculpting 64

    Hollow-constructed Harlequin 65

    Slab-built Horse 69

The Potter's Wheel 74

    How to Throw a Wide-necked Bowl . . 76

    How to Throw a Small Bowl 83

Decorating Your Ware 84

    Using an Airbrush 94

How to Use Glazes 98

Kilns 108

Firing the Ware 116

SPECIAL FEATURES:

    How to Pour a Mold 122

    How to Throw and Decorate a Vase . 130

    Charcoal Bag: New Method of
        Copying 133

    Wall and Table-top Tile 136

    Liquid Mask for Decorating 140

Glossary of Ceramics Terms 141

Manufacturers of Ceramics Supplies . . . 143

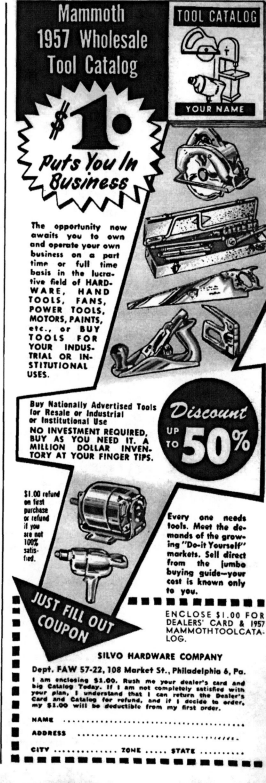

author's introduction

FOR MORE than twenty years I have been an avid and fascinated collector of ceramics. Always on the lookout for new additions to my collection, I combed the antique shops, farmhouses and auctions in small communities. Occasionally I was rewarded with a beautiful piece of bisque, a cup and saucer of Irish Baleek or perhaps a beautifully executed piece of jasper. I collected no particular period and no particular style of ware. My only rule was that the piece should be beautiful to see and crafted of excellent workmanship. A Delft windmill, a Minton moustache cup or a pitcher of Spode or Wedgwood — these to me were things of beauty and worthy of a place in my collection. It might be the glaze, the line, or the feeling that a particular piece gave me in order to merit space in my rapidly growing collection of treasures.

From this association grew the desire to create something in ceramics. Something of beauty from my own hands. I learned within a comparatively short time that anyone can make beautiful and lasting ceramic pieces with a bare minimum of tools and equipment, that manufacturers today have taken the chance out of ceramics and that many delightful and useful things can be made in the home at a fraction of their cost. I have established a studio, created my own potter's mark (see cut) and make new ceramic pieces in every spare moment. I have found a new world. If you haven't made a ceramic item yet, then I envy you your first thrill when you hold in your hand your first piece still warm from the kiln.

I want to thank the nation's ceramic manufacturers for their help in working with me to create a really easy-to-understand book embodying the basic principles of ceramics. I especially want to thank the following: Harold C. Castor of Sculptors and Ceramic Workshop in New York City; Indiana University; Karl Martz; The Metropolitan Museum of Art; J. Z. Allen; Martin Miller of Craftools; Stevens-Lapp Associates; Ed Greenstreet of Ceramichrome; Josiah Wedgwood & Sons, Inc.; Paragon Industries; D. H. C. Kilns, Inc.; L&L Manufacturing Co.; Harrop Ceramic Service Co.; Mayco Colors.

Gertrude Engel

ceramics
through the ages

The history of ceramics is a fascinating adventure into ancient cultures and into the ways in which the techniques of this art underwent refinement.

Della Robbia medallion, portraying Prudence, is enameled terra cotta made in Florence around 1455.

CERAMICS may be defined as the molding of clay or earth bodies into various plastic shapes and then using intense heat to give them permanency. It is probably the oldest of all crafts, since nothing more is needed to fashion a crude earthenware vessel than natural clay, warm sun and two hands.

Archeologists have uncovered the pottery remains of societies which antedate recorded history by hundreds of centuries. Some of these primitive jugs and bowls were made when man still did his hunting with stone axes. The ravages of time have not marred their utilitarian beauty, for when a ceramic article is fired properly it is converted into one of the most indestructible of ordinary things. When it is

5

Egyptian decorated pottery of predynastic era, before 3200 B.C.; heights are 2¾ to 12 inches.

shaped with imagination and skill, it can become a work of exquisite beauty.

Today it is possible for anyone, in his spare time, to produce eye-pleasing ceramic objects for the home—from simple ash trays to complete sets of dinnerware. With the advantages of modern technology, the do-it-yourself hobbyist can make ceramic pieces which until recently could only be turned out by the full-time professional. Best of all, perhaps, is that ceramics as a hobby is satisfying and exciting fun.

Despite the many innovations—easy-to-apply colors and glazes, electric kilns, prepared clays—enjoyed by hobbyists today, the basic methods of ceramic manufacture have not changed since the days of prehistoric man. They have been improved, embellished upon, but not essentially changed.

Of course, there is no precise history of how or when man added pottery-making to his repertoire of skills. For millions of years he used what he found lying about him, such things as seashells and gourds, to transport his precious water supply. Thus, it is not surprising that the earliest examples of earthenware are modeled after these naturally formed vessels.

In all probability, man stumbled across this revolutionary discovery as the result of some fortunate accident. Perhaps some cave children were playing by a river bank, making mud pies as youngsters still do. Maybe one inventive child shaped his mud pie after a gourd shell and left his handiwork in the sun for a few days, where it was baked into the first man-made ceramic bowl—capable of holding water.

In virtually every known primitive culture the secret of making clay pottery was known. It was learned either by word of mouth or discovered independently. The tribes-people took such clay as they could find on the surface of the ground, or by some river bed, and spread it out on stone slabs. Then they picked out the rocky fragments and beat it with the hands or sticks to fashion it into the shapes they needed or fancy dictated. For ages, the tools and techniques were of the simplest: the fingers for shaping or building up vessels and a piece of mat or basketwork on which to work.

Then some original genius of the tribe found that by turning his support he could bring every part under his hand in succession. The potter's wheel was born.

At first all pottery was hardened by drying in the sun, but the increasing use of fire soon brought out the fact that a fire-baked clay vessel becomes as hard as stone. Man had no time for luxury then; every-

thing was made strictly for utilitarian purposes. Thousands of years were to pass before he found that different districts produce different colors of clay, which led to the use of decoration.

These ancient discoveries have been the base upon which the ceramics of the last 4000 years have been built.

Pottery-making, however, did not become a complete art until the technique of glazing was mastered. Simple clay is porous after being fired—it will hold water for some time, but the liquid will leak slowly through the air spaces between the clay particles. Glazing not only made ceramics more durable and eye-worthy, but also watertight.

Glazes are superficial layers of molten material which have been fired on the clay substance. They are as varied as the many kinds of pottery, and it must never be forgotten that each type of ceramic body is at its best with its appropriate glaze.

The early Egyptians, Syrians and Persians are generally credited with developing the first practical glazing material—a very uncertain alkaline. Pioneer pottery-makers found that glazes often changed the natural clay colors. They gradually learned to use iron, manganese and cobalt to tint their wares with breath-taking results. Some of the earliest glazes were colored

New Year's bottle is Egyptian faience of Saite period, between the years of 663 and 525 B.C.

7

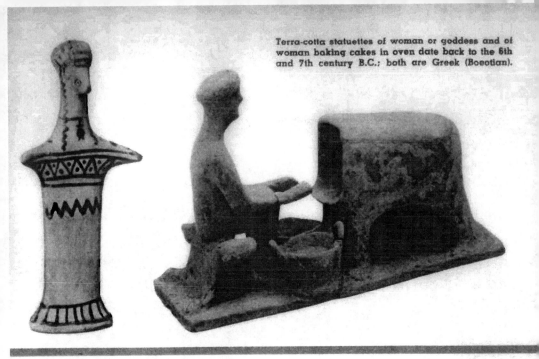

Terra-cotta statuettes of woman or goddess and of woman baking cakes in oven date back to the 6th and 7th century B.C.; both are Greek (Boeotian).

glass containing copper or iron which produced elegant green, turquoise and yellow vases of ancient Egyptian and Assyrian origin.

Marvelous work was wrought with these few materials, but the era of truly fine pottery dawned with the Persian, Egyptian and Syrian work that immediately preceded the Crusades.

By this time, the art of glazing pottery with a clear soda-lime had been thoroughly learned by Middle East artisans. This permitted a new and revolutionary coloring technique known as *under-glazing*—that is, the painting of pottery decorations before the glaze is fired. After being removed from the kiln, the designs could be seen in radiant hues, glowing through the transparent glaze.

Vases, tiles, oil lamps and ceremonial plates, shaped in good plastic clay, were covered with a white silicous coating, fit to receive glazes of this kind, giving the best possible ground for the painted colors then known.

While Middle East ceramists were producing their beautiful masterpieces, other cultures throughout the world were also experimenting, creating new and wondrous works of art from clay and fire. Just as the potter's wheel was discovered independently by many races, so was the use of molds and liquefied clay, known today as *slip*.

First to make extensive use of molds were the Greeks, who also developed the use of naturalistic painted decoration. In the Golden Age of Greece, the art of the ceramic painter was so far separated from that of the potter that each was able to put his signature on his portion of the work. The best examples of early Greek pottery often bear the marks of two master craftsmen.

At about 1000 B.C., there was a tremendous upheaval in Greek art. The geometric style of linear decoration—crowded ornamentation with repeated rows of figures, triangles, lozenges, circles and zigzags—characterize Grecian ceramics of this period. Many of the designs were entirely local. The most elaborate were those of Athens, called Diplynware after the cemetery at the city gate, where the largest vases have been found. There are huge sepulchral jars which bear among the geometric patterns, panels filled with pictures of funerals, corpses surrounded by mourners, and processions of chariots. The stylized human and animal figures were drawn in stark, dramatic, black silhouette.

The next significant developments took place in Italy, after Greece fell to the invading legions of Rome. In the centuries that followed, Greek influence was extremely potent in all Roman art because so many workmen were imported either as colonists or slaves. Much early Italian

Graceful Mesopotamian jug and vases date back to 11th to 13th centuries. Jug is unglazed, the vase at right is lustered faience.

pottery can be distinguished from the Greek only by a slight difference in the clay.

But Rome was to develop its own ceramic art.

The first pure Italian pottery was created from a bright red clay still found in the south of the peninsula. When ornamented, the works were molded with reliefs. Their almost dazzling luster was produced with a thin alkaline glaze which gave an extraordinary depth and richness to the clay colors. The earliest decoration—predominantly floral patterns, masks, dances, feasts, battles and other episodes of life— was copied heavily from the embossed silverware looted and brought back from Alexandria by Roman soldiers.

Almost from the start, Roman potters cast their works in clay molds, which were prepared mechanically by means of separate stamps. The final artistic effect was therefore dependent upon the potter's imagination and skill.

At about 100 A.D., the Italian art was suddenly eclipsed by the delicate ceramic pieces made in France. Rome still produced its own coarse pottery for ordinary domestic use, unglazed and undecorated, which formed the bulk of ancient ceramics of all periods. But the wealthy class, for whom all fine pottery was manufactured, was won over by the superior craftsmanship and quality offered by the Gallic pot-

ters. The colors were more vivid and the clay-paste itself was harder and more durable. Examples of this pottery, called Sigillata, are still excavated all over the Roman world, but most abundantly in central France.

An important technical development of the 2nd century was relief applied in *barbotine,* slip laid on by piping, which seems to have been a German innovation. (Today this technique is known as *slip-trailing.*) It was also about this time that lead glazes came into widespread use.

Until the 15th century, there was little advancement in ceramic technique throughout Europe. The Dark Ages were particularly dim in connection with pottery-making. Vessels were made for use and not for show. They were clumsily fashioned of any local clay, and if glazed at all then only with coarse lead glazes colored dull yellow or green. In no case was the workmanship above the level of the itinerant brick- or tile-maker. The best work of this 1300-year drought is found in the Gothic tile pavements of France, Germany and England.

As early as the 12th century, however, the superior artistic pottery of the Moslem nations attracted the notice of Europeans as an article of luxury for the rich. Saracen potters were often imported and patronized by wealthy connoisseurs in Italy and France.

9

Italian maiolica bowl from 15th century is deep, with vertical collar and flaring rim, and on foot.

Nearly foot-high Italian maiolica cup was made in Faenza in the late 15th or early 16th century.

When the Moors crossed from North Africa into Spain in the 11th century, they brought with them the know-how which was to make the Iberian Peninsula the ceramic center of the western world. References are found in the writings of the next three centuries to the "golden pottery" of Aragon and Granada. This refers to the lustrous tin-enameled earthenware, painted in metallic colors derived from silver and copper, which is the most famous of the Moorish-Spanish pottery.

In later times the site of manufacture passed to Valencia, from where in the 15th century gorgeous ceramic articles were exported to such distant places as London, Cairo and the Crimea. Potters from every kingdom in Europe pilgrimaged to Spain to learn the secrets introduced by the Moors.

Those who learned best, perhaps, were the Italians. The Renaissance was blossoming forth; all forms of Italian art were progressed—painting, sculpture and architecture as well as ceramics. And the Italian pottery of the early Renaissance represented the highest achievement of the potter's art in Europe.

These fine Italian wares are mostly of the type known as maiolica—earthenware coated with an opaque tin glaze or enamel as a ground for painted decoration. The name comes from the island of Majorca and was originally a misnomer.

All the beautiful and highly valued Spanish ceramics imported into Italy arrived on Majorcan trading ships. The Italians mistakenly supposed that the pottery was manufactured in Majorca, when actually it was made on the Spanish mainland. They named it accordingly. When local imitations sprang up in Italy, they were also called maiolica. The name stuck to the new tin-enamel ware which was introduced at the dawn of the Renaissance.

In spite of its beauty, maiolica was soon surpassed in popularity by still another new kind of ceramic ware. If ever there was a revolution in the history of ceramics it was late in the 15th century, after Marco Polo pioneered the first trading route to China and the Far East. Europe was agog over the wondrous commodities arriving on merchants ships from the Orient—silks and spices and exotic new fragrances. And a remarkable, smooth, glistening, translucent form of pottery.

This most exquisite of man-made ceramics was named by some unknown Italian shell worker in the early 1600's, who stood on a wharf in Venice watching the sailors unload a cargo of Chinese wares. Admiring the fine workmanship evidenced by the vases and statuettes, he likened the shape of one lustrous variety to a little pig, which in Italian is translated into *porzellana*. Today we call it porcelain.

The history of Oriental pottery-making,

Stamped terra-cotta tile is Chinese piece from Han Dynasty, dating from 206 B.C. to 220 A.D.

for the most part, is much like that of the rest of the world. Improvements were made gradually over thousands of years, although the Japanese and Chinese apparently got a head-start in the field.

As early as 3000 B.C., Chinese ceramists were shaping some of the most artistic pottery in the annals of man. Europe at this date was still the home of roving bands of barbarians, who knew little more about making pottery than their earliest forebears.

Probably the most august age of Chinese ceramics was during the Sung Dynasty, which lasted from 960-1279 A.D. It was in this period that porcelain was first developed. The earliest known examples of porcelain are of the *ying ch'ing* type—a soft-looking, bubbly glaze, white in color but with a faint tinge of iridescent green or blue.

Chinese artisans jealously guarded their individual techniques for producing porcelain. The clay had to be properly aged, in many cases for centuries. Succeeding generations of potters inherited the family's supply of clay, which was buried in the ground to be dug up more than 100 years later by a potter's son or grandson.

Chinese pilgrim bottle of white clay stands 15 inches high; from T'ang dynasty, 618-906 A.D.

Head of Kuan Yin is porcelain, 7 inches high, dating to Yüan dynasty in China, years 1280 to 1368.

German drinking vessel in form of owl bears Hohenzollern arms, is 16½ inches high; dates 1550-1600. Center, ewer of Chinese porcelain from Wan Li period (1575-1619) was decorated with English mounts. Delft faience vase by Van Eenhoorn, about 1700, is one of pair, has polychrome decoration on white.

When Oriental porcelain was introduced into Europe in the 15th century, it made even the most beautiful of western pottery look shabby by comparison. European ceramists regarded the Chinese—and later, Japanese—wares with awe and envy. Ambitious efforts were made to imitate the imported porcelain, which was in heavy demand among wealthy collectors. When Italian potters took to coating their earthenwares with white enamel, which gave a superficial porcelain look, it was only the first of a long list of dismal failures.

The problem soon attracted the attention of Italian majolists and alchemists. The first reasonable imitation of porcelain was made at Florence in 1585 by a team of alchemists and potters working under the patronage of Francesco de Medici.

This Florentine "porcelain" was the forerunner of many European wares made in avowed imitation of true Oriental porcelain. They form a link between pottery and glass, for they may be considered either as pottery rendered translucent or as glass rendered opaque by shaping and firing a mixture containing a large percentage of glass with small amounts of clay.

But the search for the secret of true porcelain manufacture was excitedly continued by European ceramists for generations. The imitations ran the gamut of invention and ingenuity. By the mid-17th century, the research was considered so important that the experimenters, backed by such patrons as the Elector of Saxony and Madame de Pompadour, were more interested in solving the riddle of porcelain than they were in the transmutation of base metals into gold.

Although many of the imitations resembled porcelain at first glance, all of them were made of soft-paste clays. It remained for a German named Johannes Boettger to turn out the first true European porcelain in the year 1709.

By experiments with the fusing of clays, Boettger discovered the secret of making a high-fired mixture of fusible and nonfusible silicates of alumina, called by the Chinese *petuntse* and *kaolin*, and in English china-stone and china-clay.

Boettger was first to realize that Chinese porcelain could be made with potter's material alone. Because of its translucence, other experimenters were certain the Chinese had mixed glass with clay. In effect, as Boettger proved, they did. The Orientals, however, instead of fusing finished glass with clay, fused the raw ingredients.

From Boettger's factory at Meissen sprang others making hard-paste porcelain comparable with the Chinese and Japanese.

Another Delft faience piece of about 1700, plate above bears Japanese Imari decoration in colors and gold on white ground; made by P. Adriaensz.

Slipware plate of red earthenware is an American piece probably made by Henry Roudeburth, Montgomery County, Pennsylvania; signed date: 1793.

The spread of European porcelain-making, though, was relatively slow, since the manufacturers attempted to monopolize the secrets of their trade. Competing potters were not above hiring spies in each other's potteries to snoop for secrets. We are told, for example, that the brothers Elers in England employed none but deaf mutes at the Staffordshire plant, to prevent their techniques from leaking out to competitors.

Both by spying and by independent discovery, the secret of making genuine porcelain was known in virtually every European country by the end of the 19th century. It was the dawn of a new golden age in European ceramics. Names like Wedgwood, Spode, Delft, Minton, Irish Beleek and Meissen became synonymous with fine china. These famed manufactories are a fascinating study in themselves.

Modern science has removed the aura of secrecy which once surrounded ceramics. Today the tyro ceramists, in their own kitchen, can produce the most beautiful objects with little difficulty. More and more people are indulging their desire for self-expression through this medium. They are finding how easy it is to make fine pottery inexpensively and enjoyably. Save for the hobbyist's own imagination, there is virtually no limit to what can be done—by *you*. •

Mexican maiolica lavatory of about 1830 was made for Franciscan church in Puebla, is 8 feet long.

Brown glaze pottery jug is 19th century American (probably from Ohio); its height is 7⅝ inches.

ceramics as a hobby

One of the nation's favorite pastimes, ceramics offers both excitement and practical uses.

IN THE COLD, concise language of Webster's Dictionary, clay is "an earthy substance used in making pottery, bricks, etc." To the ceramist this definition seems much too objective and academic—like saying the Hope Diamond is nothing more than a chunk of carbon which has undergone immense subterranean pressure and heat. Surely this flawless gem is worthy of a more full-flavored description.

So it is with clay. It can be shaped, colored and fired into myriad marvels of esthetic and utilitarian beauty. It has "life" and is capable of playing strange tricks under the influence of fire. Colors, too, are often capricious. Even under the strictest control they may effect results which are, to say the least, unexpected.

Every time you open the kiln, it's like Christmas. For you can never be certain about exactly what you'll get. These surprise endings only add an extra dash of spice to an already absorbing hobby.

When you have started to work with ceramics, you will find that the more you know, the more there is to learn about this fascinating creative art. As with any worthwhile accomplishment, you will not become an expert potter merely by reading a book.

Photos of finished pieces courtesy Sculptors and Ceramic Workshop

You will have to taste your share of joys and disappointments during your trial-and-error apprenticeship. But don't be too easily discouraged if at first your trials turn out to be mostly errors.

Most educators agree that lessons learned by trial and error are lessons best remembered. With ceramics, moreover, all mistakes are not for the worst. On the contrary, many of a potter's errors result in his most attractive and original works. Usually these are the pieces which can never be duplicated.

Very popular in the ceramist's lexicon of phrases are the words "let's see what happens." The thrill of experimentation is not lacking in this hobby. For example, you could glaze a tray and toss on a few pieces of copper, just to "see what happens." After firing it, you may find the copper completely burned away, leaving a scrumptious splotch of green from the copper oxide. On the other hand, the copper might scale over the glaze and ruin the tray. You won't know until you remove it from the kiln—and the suspense, as any ceramics enthusiast knows, can be unbearable.

Since the end of World War II, ceramics has mushroomed in popularity until today it is one of the nation's favorite pastimes. Its enthusiastic adherents are outnumbered, according to latest estimates, only by those of bowling, fishing and stamp collecting. As for *creative* hobbies, there are more ceramists in the country than any other breed of amateur artist.

Actually, it is difficult to put your finger on the reason for this sudden spurt in popularity. Perhaps it can be attributed to the war itself. Existing conditions then made it impossible to import pottery from abroad. Stores were eager to sell locally made merchandise. Critical shortages existed in metals and other materials that normally go into gift ware. But there has always been an abundance of raw material for the manufacture of pottery: clay. And the metallic oxides and carbonates that are used for pottery colors were likewise available throughout the war years.

Americans are traditionally an enterprising people and it was only natural that hundreds of small potteries developed into lucrative businesses overnight. Many ceramists joined the bonanza with little more experience than a correspondence course in pottery-making and a few hundred dollars in capital.

Above, class of ceramic hobby beginners work with factory-prepared greenware which sells for as little as 35 cents; adjoining photo shows hobbyist using small kiln, costing only about $20, to fire work.

Where formerly a potter had to possess the technical skills of a chemist and an engineer to work out formulas for clay bodies and glazes, it was suddenly possible in most cities to buy prepared clays and glazes with easy-to-follow directions. As a result, in the past dozen or so years, American-made ceramics have so improved in quality and craftsmanship that many domestic wares have equalled, if not surpassed, those of famous and respected Old World potteries.

The application of modern science has removed every trace of drudgery from the ceramic art. It has been distilled into pure fun. Youngsters are being taught ceramics in thousands of schools. Oldsters are converting their sewing machines into potter's wheels for throwing hand-turned pieces. In garages, basements, porches, kitchens, millions of spare-time ceramists are enjoying the pleasant sensation of creating something and then seeing their creations finished in practical, permanent form.

Even the making of a simple pot or bowl, which is not beyond the ken of anyone, is a soul-satisfying experience. Expensive equipments and superior artistic talent are not needed. There is room in this field for every kind of expression. You may enjoy sculpting most, or making jewelry, or painting china. Or maybe you will just want to let your imagination show you the way.

An entire book could be filled just by listing the variety of things which can be made with clay. There are the obvious projects, such as teapots, vases, banks and beer mugs, which usually represent a point of departure for most beginners. But there are other less common ceramic objects—doorknobs, comb tops, chessmen, buttons. Even tile swimming pools!

Some ceramists have used their hobby as a means for keeping a permanent record

personal touch that will be treasured by the lucky recipients.

When the holidays arrive, you will be able to add lots of extra highlights to your family's enjoyment.

Christmas? Well, you can make unique ornaments for the tree and outstanding table decorations that will enhance any Yule turkey: Santa Clauses, reindeer, holy figurines, wreaths, and so forth.

You can, if you wish to do something rather spectacular, make your Christmas cards on tile with a personalized greeting to the special people in your life. This will be one Yule card they won't discard after New Year's Day. For one thing, it can handily be utilized as a hot-plate if the addressee has a practical turn of mind.

Easter again offers the opportunity for adding eye-appeal to the dinner table, with ceramic bunnies, chicks and egg baskets. If you want to delight the youngsters in your household, make them a few dozen Easter eggs in your ceramic workshop. Valentine's Day, Fourth of July and Halloween also offer opportunities for showing off your clay-working prowess.

Need a new lamp in the living room? Instead of shopping around and hoping that you'll find something which only resembles what you desire, make it yourself. It's not hard, really, once you have mastered the basic techniques of making ceramic wares. Once started, you'll find no end of things

Right, modernistic piece combines ovoid vase with decor of stylized fish; avoid photo-like realism.

of their children's development. The kindergarten boy or girl brings home drawings made on cheap paper which in a few years crumble into dust, much to the parent's dismay. However, if these same drawings, so much treasured by parents, were done on tile, they would never fade; the colors would remain vivid and fresh as the day they were made.

Among the most popular do-it-yourself projects today is the tile-topped coffee table. In a fine furniture shop such a table would cost an absolute minimum of $100. Yet, the ceramics hobbyist in his spare time can produce just as fine a table quite simply and at one-fourth the price.

Similarly, when gift-giving time rolls around, you can present your family and friends with things no one else could possibly give them—things you have created especially for each of them. Your gifts, though inexpensive to make, will bear the

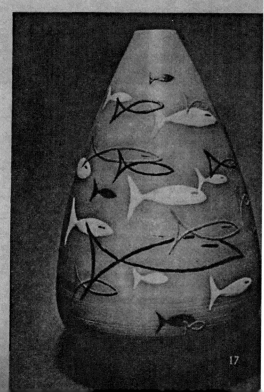

which can be made for the home and your own personal adornment. The most ordinary article can be given real, lasting beauty with a bit of imagination on the ceramist's part.

Take, as an example, a commonplace kitchen knife. Let's say the handle is broken. The blade, however, is fine steel and it would be a shame to throw it away. For the ceramist, this is no problem. Rather, it's an *opportunity*. All that need be done is to make another handle out of clay, striving, of course, to make it handsomer than the original.

These are but a few of the things you can accomplish after gaining a little background knowledge and practical experience. Stop and think for a few minutes and you'll be able to come up with many, many others.

Just to run through the alphabet, there are: ash trays, bells, cigarette boxes, dresser sets, egg cups, figurines, gravy dishes, hat pins, inkwells, jam jars, lockets, mirror frames, napkin rings, ocarinas, pipe holders, quatrefoil wall plaques, razor holders, saltcellars, thimbles, umbrella handles, vases, window boxes, Yule cards, zipper tags for children which bear the wearer's name and address.

You could probably compile a similar list in short order. Perhaps, you'll even think of a ceramic something that begins with the letter X. Many ceramists have turned their hobby into profitable sidelines by conceiving of new ceramic forms.

The vast majority of professional clay workers today got their start as amateur hobbyists, just like you. After they advanced far enough, they found that people

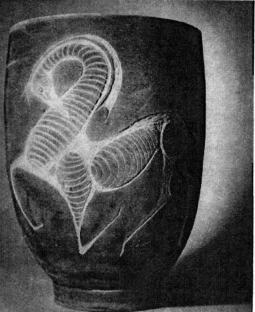

Beautiful candlesticks with tear-drop motif of black underglaze over white ceramic body could have been glazed in high-gloss finish if desired.

Squat white-body clay vase was textured on wheel with use of rough-edged clay-working tool; top and bottom were smoothed, center decorated.

Sgraffito technique to produce stylized horse on stoneware vase was combined with textured background; many objects can be used to add texture.

There's no reason why you cannot turn your pastime into a profitable venture. However, unless you are some sort of wizard, the likes of which has yet to be discovered, it will be only after several years of practice. Though you may produce a perfect example of ceramic art on your very first attempt, which is not unusual, it requires study, patience and diligent application to do it time after time.

Besides gaining the sure-handed technique required of the professional, you will also have to develop the spark of inventive ability exhibited by the pace-setters in every field of endeavor. There is one more prerequisite for professionalism, by far the most important: You must get genuine pleasure from working with clay. If you do, there is a good chance that in the future you will be able to pad your regular income by selling the products of your studio.

The primary objective of most beginners, though, is to have fun and at the same time create fine ceramic items to enrich their homes. If this is your main target, you will find this a fascinating, rewarding pastime. Best of all, you'll be amazed at how soon you are turning out work you will be proud to show off.

This book is intended to be a guide for those who want to learn about ceramics for their own pleasure, first. The problems which are most likely to be puzzling to the tyro will be explained in pictures and down-to-earth language.

Step by step, you will learn about the tools and materials you will need; about molds, kilns, the potter's wheel, colors and glazes. You will be introduced to the various types of ceramics and learn the techniques in making each. You will learn how to plan and furnish your ceramics workshop. Finally, throughout the pages of this book are special do-it-yourself projects explained in detail, and most of these can be handled competently by the beginner. Let's get started. •

were willing to pay for the ceramic goods they produced.

Of course it is nice to be able to make your hobby pay for itself. And it's even nicer if you can earn a living by doing something you enjoy. Many part-time potters entered the professional ranks when they found there was a market for molds of their original wares. Other hobbyists wanted to duplicate the pieces and they were willing to pay for the molds in which to cast them.

Besides selling their creations and the molds thereof, many professionals gain added income by teaching classes. Besides the tuition, which is generally very modest, they sell the necessary supplies to their students, and *greenware*, which are unfired pieces ready to be decorated, glazed and placed in the kiln.

how to start: your tools

The wise way is to start slowly, to save money and avoid confusion. You'll

THERE is a vast variety of tools and equipment now available to the ceramics hobbyist. Suppliers' catalogues are jam-packed with paraphernalia for the amateur workshop. After paging through one of these catalogues, the beginner is apt to be overimpressed with the necessity for fancy tools and equipment. Fact is, however, that very few implements are can't-do-withouts for the beginning ceramist.

A working surface covered with a piece of oilcloth, wrong side up; one or two simple modeling tools, a knife, and about five pounds of clay are all you need to start shaping your first object. The cost of these is negligible. Most clays, for example, can be bought from retail dealers at about 15 cents a pound.

Build your collection of tools slowly, adding items as you need them. It is likely that you will do your first clay-craft in a local studio or classroom, under the guidance of a professional teacher. It is not probable that you'll begin sculpting or casting your own pieces in a mold. Instead, you will be supplied with greenware, a

fettling knife, brushes, colors and glazes. You will remove the mold marks from the greenware, smooth the surface, add some decoration and glaze. Then the professional ceramist will fire it for you in his kiln.

After you have learned to do this, which shouldn't take more than one or two lessons, you may want to take the greenware home and finish it there. In all likelihood, you will buy the few necessary tools from your teacher. This will be the start of your own home workshop.

Of course many new ceramists begin by immediately furnishing a complete studio, from clay to kiln. In most cases this is not advisable for two reasons. First, there are financial considerations which would frustrate this grandiose plan of action for most people. Second, it is more prudent to wait and see what type of equipment is best suited to your personal needs and desires. The clay worker who wants to specialize in hand-sculpture will not require the very same tools and materials as the one whose skills and fancy lean toward pottery.

When you select a site for your workshop, make certain it is not exposed di-

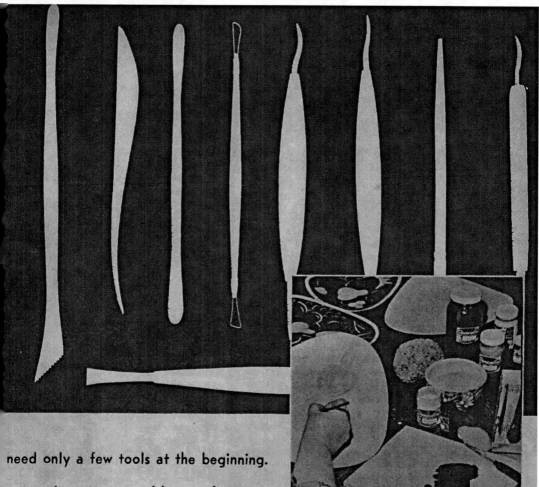

need only a few tools at the beginning.

rectly to extremes of heat or dampness. Good lighting is also important, contributing both to the ceramist's comfort and to the quality of his work. Running water, or easy access to water, is also desirable. Until you start to accumulate a sizable collection of tools and equipment, and want to set up your own workshop, your kitchen should serve the purpose.

Many tools you will be able to make easily for yourself; others you will find already at hand about the house. No matter how far you advance in the ceramics art, you'll find the most useful tools are your fingers. Every other modeling device is employed simply to supplement the work that can be done with your hands. When shaping a piece of clay, tools will only assist your fingers. They will not accomplish anything that can't be done with your fingers.

Equipping Your Workshop

Here's a list of materials you will find useful in your workshop: an inexpensive rolling pin which can be purchased at most chain stores and toy shops; pie plates;

One of your first projects will be decorating of greenware (see page 68), requiring little more than glazed tile, sponge, brushes, colors (those in photo are Ceramichrome). Below, to scratch a design through slip, sgraffito tools are used.

Leveling screen made of grit cloth tacked over plywood is used to level base of any greenware rubbed over it, to prevent "rock."

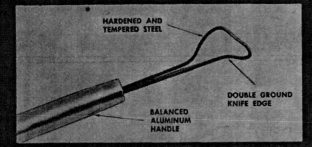

HARDENED AND TEMPERED STEEL

DOUBLE GROUND KNIFE EDGE

BALANCED ALUMINUM HANDLE

Above, synthetic sponges, silk sponge at top right, elephant-ear sponge beneath.

Left, closeup of Craftool modeling and carving tool. See photo of set, right.

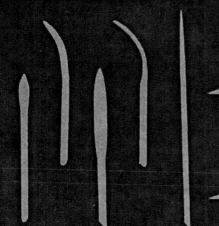

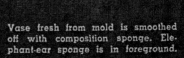

Buy good brushes for good work. A selection of soft sable brushes is needed. Pointed one is for engobes.

Vase fresh from mold is smoothed off with composition sponge. Elephant-ear sponge is in foreground.

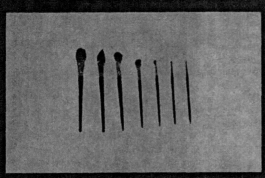

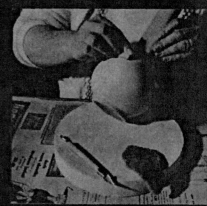

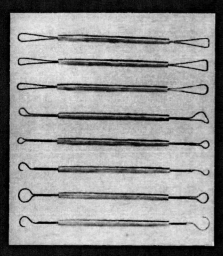

Eight-piece set of modeling and carving
tools made by Craftools cost $6 to $10.

Metal scrapers made in both a kidney and
rectangular shape are used for leveling
and creating textured effects in the ware.

toothpicks; building plaster; an orange
stick; a piece of ordinary, unsoaped steel
wool; a sheet of grade 00 sandpaper; a
paring knife; a scraper or spatula; a coarse
sponge and a small facial sponge; some
crocks or large Mason jars. You probably
have most of these things already in the
home.

A plastic or crockery pitcher will also
find use in the workshop, as will a galva-
nized pail and a few cheap mixing bowls.
If a pitcher is not readily available, you
can substitute a large tin can with a
lacquered inner surface. By pinching the
rim of the lidless can, you will form a
pouring spout.

If you plan to do much work with solid
clay, it will be worth while to make yourself
a wedging wire. Before clay is shaped it
must always be wedged. This is a method
of mixing a mass of clay thoroughly by
cutting it in half and slamming the two
pieces together on the work surface with
the cut edges in opposite directions. This is
done in order to remove all air pockets
and holes which would cause a piece to
explode when fired, and to secure an even
consistency.

A wedging wire is used to slice blocks
of clay into two. Of course a knife can be
used, but not as handily or effectively.
This device is easily constructed by attaching dowel handles to the ends of a 12-inch
piano wire, about 18 gauge.

The more ambitious ceramist can go a
step further and build a *wedging board,*
which serves the same purpose but is a
more permanent fixture in the workshop.
You can make a simple one by constructing a 6-inch deep wooden box measuring
about 15x26 inches, and fastening at the
back an upright post measuring about
1x2x18 inches. At the top of the vertical
rod, secure a piece of non-rusting wire, not
thinner than 12 gauge. The other end of
the wire is stretched to the front of the box
and fastened taut. Use a turnbuckle or a
wingnut to tighten the wire.

The wedging board should be weighted
by filling the box with plaster (mixed, perhaps, with gravel or small rocks). When
using the board to cut clay, always start
under the wire and draw the clay toward
you. Thus, any bit of clay flicked out by
the wire will be thrown away from you
rather than hitting you in the face.

For decorating purposes, you will need
several soft-hair brushes with which to
apply colors and glazes. These can also be
used for applying liquid clay (or *slip*), for
mending and general modeling or shaping
purposes. The brushes can be of average

23

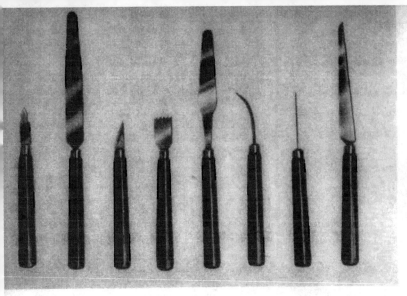

Ceramic scraper and texturing set has sgraffito scraper, palette knives, angle scraper knife, texturing tool, curved scraper, needle tool, and a fettling knife; price is under $4.

quality, such as imitation camel's-hair watercolor brushes. Both pointed and flat-tipped brushes should be in supply. Numbers 3, 5, 8 and 10 will serve almost all requirements.

Wooden modeling tools also simplify the shaping and decorating of a clay object. It is easier to push the clay into rough form with a mallet or a block of wood than with the fist or the heel of the hand. After the roughing-out has been completed and the large masses are shaped, more detailed modeling begins. This calls for a few wooden modeling sticks about 6 to 8 inches long, with thin, flat blades. The blade ends are used for cutting, smoothing and shaping surfaces and for welding fine lines. The round ends are used for welding coils together and for all-around modeling and shaping.

A scratch-point is helpful in etching designs in a clay body. Almost anything with a sharp point can be used effectively—an orange stick or any piece of doweling which has been sharpened to a point. You can, if you wish, buy metal scratch-points in most stationery stores. These will fit into any penholder. If you want to do sgraffito work—decorations formed by cutting or scratching through an outer coating of slip to show the clay underneath—a scratch-point is a handy implement.

As you progress and want to try new decorating methods, you'll probably attempt slip-trailing, a method by which you achieve designs in relief. Slip-trailing is much like decorating a cake with the words "happy birthday." A hand irrigating syringe with a hard-rubber nozzle and a bulb can be used for this technique. Cost is less than a dollar in the local drugstore.

Wire-loop tools always find their way into the ceramist's workshop because of the varied uses to which they can be put. Again, they are valuable tools for carving sgraffito designs. Also they are used for smoothing the surface of pottery and sculpture, especially for cutting down high places and for hollowing out hand-shaped figurines before firing. Select three or more loop tools of sizes varying from 8 to 10 inches long, and with different shaped loops.

When working with molded greenware, you will need a fettling knife and/or an elephant sponge to sand off the mold marks and to smooth surfaces and edges. Cellulose sponges or fine sandpaper can also be utilized.

Plaster Bats

Although oilcloth is a satisfactory work surface for the beginner, a plaster *bat* is much more desirable. It not only provides a sturdier support, but it also keeps objects moist while you are working on them. Unglazed biscuit tiles, 4x4 and 6x6 inches, are adequate for most projects. They may be purchased from a ceramics supply house for a few cents apiece.

Plaster bats are easy to make yourself. This is a valuable project for the beginner because it provides a background of experience for casting and mold-making. Bats can be made in any size, and a variety of sizes are needed.

A 12-inch pie plate makes an ideal mold for a round plaster bat. The first step in making such a bat is to fill a container with the amount of water that the pie plate will

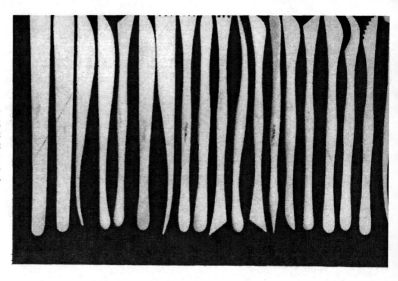

Set of twenty wood modeling tools of polished hardwood come in plastic kit, cost about $6.50. Both this set and one shown on the facing page are made by Craftools, Inc. Refer to pages 143, 144.

hold. Add powdered plaster of Paris and stir to a molasses consistency. The liquid plaster is now poured into the pie-plate mold. Agitate the plate gently to free the plaster of air bubbles. At least 24 hours will be required for the plaster to set and dry properly.

You follow the same instructions for making a square bat, but instead of using a pie plate you use a square form, perhaps a medium-size cardboard box.

The plaster bat is a porous platform on which you can work. By sprinkling it with water as you work, you can keep the piece on which you're working in a moist, plastic state for a long period of time. By the same token, a bat can be used for the reverse purpose—to dry a piece of clay which is too moist for immediate work. The porous surface will extract excess moisture from the clay.

Other Materials

A whirler or banding wheel is also a sound investment for the ceramist who has advanced far enough to furnish his own studio. Primarily such a wheel is used for decorating pottery. The top turns freely and so makes it possible for you to rotate your work constantly. By holding a paint-brush against the surface as it spins, you can paint straight and even bands of color on such things as vases and mugs. A whirler can also double as a small potter's wheel for forming pottery pieces and small ceramic figures.

After you have reached the stage where you have made or acquired your own molds, you will need an assortment of heavy rubber bands to hold together multi-pieced molds while casting greenware. Cutting cross-sections out of old, discarded innertubes should supply you with more than enough.

Your studio should also have the afore-mentioned crocks or large glass jars for holding moist clay and slip. The one-gallon jars used for packing pickles can be utilized for this purpose.

A sieve is also among the much-used workshop implements. The obvious use of the sieve is to strain partially hardened lumps and impurities from slip before pouring it into a mold.

Closely resembling the strainer is the scratch-box, which is used for a much different purpose: to level the irregular edges of pottery. A scratch-box can be quickly made by nailing together four 18-inch boards to form a box. Across the top, tack down a sheet of grit cloth. By holding a piece of greenware perpendicular to the cloth abrasive, and carefully rubbing it across the surface, you can even up the bottoms and tops of pottery.

If you want to get the most out of your tools, you should take good care of them. Keep them clean. Don't leave them soaking in water but wipe them with a damp cloth and then dry thoroughly. Metal tools should periodically be wiped with an oil-soaked cloth to prevent rusting. Plaster surfaces such as bats and wedging boards should be kept dry and clean. When you are through with them, you should wipe them dry with a damp sponge to remove clay particles.

All tools deserve good treatment and any ceramist worthy of the name has as much respect for his tools as for the clay. •

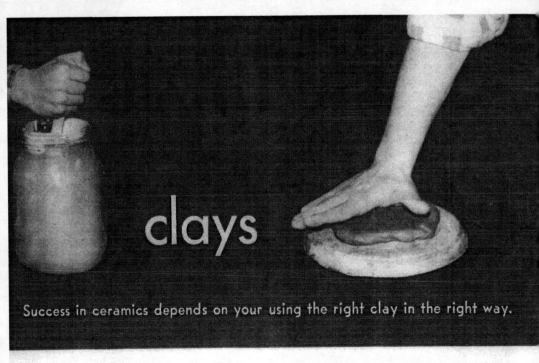

clays

Success in ceramics depends on your using the right clay in the right way.

CLAY is among the most abundant of earth's natural resources, as well as one of the cheapest and most useful. There are many different kinds of clays, natural and synthetic, used for different purposes in ceramic work. Before you begin shaping your first piece of pottery, you should know certain facts about the properties of the various clays you will use. To begin with, you should always make sure that you have chosen the right clay for each project. Needless to say, it is quite discouraging to find a piece ruined in the kiln because you used the wrong kind of clay.

Some purists suggest that you dig and prepare your own clay. Although this might be fascinating fun, it certainly is not for the beginner. Also, it is unnecessary work, since you can buy prepared clay for only a few cents a pound. If you plan to use the clay for modeling, you can purchase it already mixed and seasoned, ready for use. If you plan to use the clay for casting, that also can be bought already prepared, but since it is liquid and sold by weight, it may seem extravagant to pay for so much water.

Modeling clay is called *plastic*; clay used for casting, or pouring into molds, is referred to as *slip*. How you plan to use the clay will determine which you purchase, although one type can actually serve both purposes, the main difference being in the mixing and preparation.

When you buy clay, always be sure to ask the dealer about its firing range. Some clays do not mature unless they are fired at very high temperatures, while others will disintegrate if fired too high. The same dealer who sells you the clay can also advise you about which types of glaze to use on it.

Rarely is clay found completely free of impurities. The most common of these are sand, lime carbonate, iron sulphide and organic matter. These impurities cause variations in the color and texture of the clay. Most pure clays lack many desirable properties which have to be supplied by adding ingredients to them. If you found a pure clay plastic enough to shape into a piece of pottery, you would probably be dismayed to find it shrink excessively under fire, causing the model to warp and crack.

Two minerals which must be added to pure clay are flint and feldspar. Flint, which is silica, is employed to control shrinkage and to open the clay body when fired, permitting moisture and gases to escape. Feldspar makes the clay fuse properly at the desired temperature.

Talc is also added to many clays, especially if they are to be used for casting figurines. This is done to prevent shrinkage and also to lessen the tendency to craze. (*Crazing* refers to the tiny cracks which appear in a glaze when it does not fit the clay.)

To lower the maturing point of a clay,

ground glass is sometimes mixed into the body.

To strengthen a clay, or to reduce its tendency to crack, a *grog* may be added. Grog is composed of fired clay which has been ground into small particles. Sand or powdered quartz can also be utilized effectively as clay strengtheners.

Nowadays the hobbyist need not be bothered with the complicated details of preparing his own clays. Most dealers stock a large variety, either ready-mixed to a plastic consistency or ready for the hobbyist to mix with water and wedge to the consistency he requires.

Best known of the commercial grades of clay are ball clay, china clay and fire clay.

Ball clay is highly plastic and can easily be shaped by hand. It fuses at a fairly high temperature and is used in the manufacture of all kinds of pottery, chinaware and stoneware. England, Kentucky, Tennessee and Florida supply some of the finest ball clays.

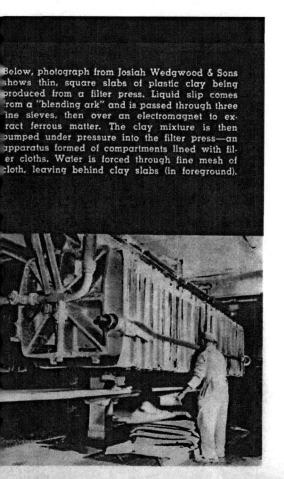

Below, photograph from Josiah Wedgwood & Sons shows thin, square slabs of plastic clay being produced from a filter press. Liquid slip comes from a "blending ark" and is passed through three fine sieves, then over an electromagnet to extract ferrous matter. The clay mixture is then pumped under pressure into the filter press—an apparatus formed of compartments lined with filter cloths. Water is forced through fine mesh of cloth, leaving behind clay slabs (in foreground).

China clay, otherwise known as kaolin, is the purest known form of clay. High-quality china clay is abundant in England and is exported extensively. In this country, Georgia is the prime source of supply. Kaolin is the only type of raw, pure clay the hobbyist should purchase for starting. This is because it has so many uses. To mention only a few, kaolin is utilized in making most glazes; it can be used in making underglazes; it is an ingredient of kiln-wash.

Fire clay has a very high vitrification, or hardening, point. This clay is valuable in the construction of kilns and the manufacture of refractory tiles, bricks, and other objects which must be able to withstand extremely high temperatures.

For the purposes of the hobbyist, it might be advantageous to classify clays according to their ultimate purposes.

First, there is pottery clay. Probably the two kinds most used are gray stoneware and terra-cotta clay. Both will produce a good plastic, workable pottery clay. The stoneware clay fires a light buff and permits the use of lighter and more brilliant colors in glazing. The terra-cotta clay fires a reddish-brown and consequently darkens all glaze colors. This should be considered when choosing clay for a project. If both types of pottery clay can be obtained, they will increase the possibilities available in decoration and colors. Terra cotta is especially suited to sculpture, and is best left unglazed as the warm color and matte surface produce an effective appearance.

Next is sculpture clay, particularly desirable for this purpose because it is stronger, more rigid, and can take more stress and strain than other clays. It contains an addition of grog. Sculpture clay can be bought prepared or made by mixing grog—about 20% by weight—with either of the pottery clays.

Finally, there is jewelry clay. The requirements for a jewelry clay are quite different from those for pottery or sculpture clay. As the object to be made is smaller in volume, the details must be finer and sharper, the colors on the finished piece should be more vivid, and the firing temperature need not be as high. Therefore, a fine-grained white clay, with a high percentage of flint, is recommended because it gives brilliance to the glaze colors and fires at a low temperature.

Preparing and Storing Clay

Whenever possible, it is simpler to buy clay in a moist state, but it can be purchased in dry powder form and mixed as needed. This will require several days, depending on the atmosphere and the temperature of the room in which the clay is mixed.

To prepare clay from the dry powder: The powder should be spread in a sink, tub or flat pan and mixed with water to the consistency of thick molasses. All lumps should be removed by stirring. Allow water to evaporate until the clay reaches a slushy state, then spread it on plaster bats to dry. Turn and press the mass before a crust develops on either side. When it passes beyond the sticky state to a soft firmness, remove it from the bats, wedge and store it.

Clay is easier and better to use when it has aged in the damp state. This means leaving it in a damp place—a box or crock —for a period of a week to two or three months, the longer the better.

So long as the clay is moist, it is very plastic and easy to work. If it is pushed, it moves readily and stays in the new shape. If a piece of clay is added to the original piece, it is only necessary to lay it firmly in place and work it into the mass with a finger or tool. But once the clay has hardened, it is practically impossible to add moist clay to it.

Clay shrinks as it dries. Thus, when moist clay is added to the semi-dry body, the moist clay shrinks more, and the unequal shrinkage causes it to crack and peel. Good modeling clay normally shrinks about one inch to every 12 inches during the processes of drying and firing. Half the shrinkage takes place while the completed model is drying, the other half takes place in the kiln.

Slip, or liquefied clay, to be used for casting objects in molds and for modeling and decorative purposes, can also be purchased in prepared form. Basically it is clay and water with some other chemicals added to produce certain definite effects.

The chemicals used in slip are called deflocculants. The purpose of a "defloc" is to form a liquid clay without using too much water. In plain language, a deflocculant is a "water wetter." That is, a small amount of liquid is made to perform the function of a larger quantity. The principle involved is that an alkaline water can hold more clay than an acid one. It separates the clay into finer particles so that they are held in suspension or a colloidal state.

Castings can be made of slips that do not contain a defloc. But it takes far longer for the mold to absorb the extra water, and the results are rarely as satisfactory. Special casting bodies may be purchased in powder form. The amount of water to add and the directions for mixing are given by the manufacturer. Common deflocculants are potassium carbonate, sodium gallate, sodium tannate, and a combination of sodium carbonate and sodium silicate (waterglass).

If you prefer making your own casting slip, rather than buying it ready mixed, take about 10 pounds of powdered clay and add five pints of water and one teaspoon of potassium carbonate, or any other deflocculant. Mix well and let stand overnight. Stir for a few minutes each day for several days. Your greatest plague will be air bubbles, which must be removed from the slip by stirring and banging. After the slip has been seasoned for one week, strain through a 60- or 80-mesh sieve. A good slip has the consistency of honey.

Plain water-and-clay slips can be used as an adhesive material for joining two pieces of plastic or leather-hard clay. In performing such an operation, it is advisable to make your slip of the same material as your ware. Otherwise the juncture may be visible after drying and finishing. If, for example, you use a red slip for mending a white clay body, the repair

Here is the way you get sizable quantities of clay. Contained in this is clay in plastic bags.

Plastic bags prevent moisture content from escaping; keep clay in them. Shown: red and white clay.

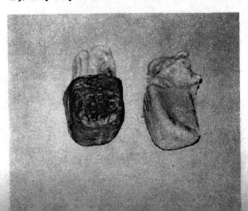

would mar the beauty of the completed piece.

For decorating, on the other hand, a contrasting slip can be used with winning results. Never slip-decorate a piece that has passed its leather-hard stage of drying, however. If the ware to be so decorated is too moist, the slip will tend to soften it. If the ware is dry-hard, you will have difficulty getting the slip to adhere properly. More than likely, the slip will chip and peel away.

Plastic clay should be kept in a container with a lid. Stoneware jars, garbage cans and laundry tubs are adaptable for this purpose. For hand-shaped pottery, the clay must be kept quite soft, not sticky, and firm, not shapeless. For sculpture, it should be stiffer so that it will not slump or sink or lose its shape.

While working on an object, the unused portion of the wedged clay should be kept under a damp cloth, or it will become too hard. If the clay is too moist, it can be rolled or wedged on a dry table or dry plaster bat until it is of the right consistency. If it is too stiff, it can be rolled or wedged on a damp surface until it is right.

To increase plasticity, you may add one of the following: acetic acid, ball clay, bentonite, dextrin, glycerine, tannic acid.

To increase the strength of clay, you may use: fire clay, flint, grog, lignin extract. (Note: Grog increases strength in dry form. The other materials weaken clay in the unfired state but increase strength after firing.)

When clay is very stiff it may be reclaimed by leaving it on a moist plaster bat, covered with a damp cloth. Clay that is bone-dry must be broken and mashed and worked like dry powder clay. It is far better to err on the side of keeping clay too wet than too dry.

Slip should always be stored in dust-tight containers. Some slips have a tendency to form a skin or crust on the top. This can partly be prevented by covering the slip pail or jar with wax paper and string.

Use Clay Properly

Craftsmanship is all-important in any part of the ceramic process. The materials can be dirty and messy—it is wise to wear an apron in the workshop—and unless a strict control is maintained over them, the results may be discouraging. Rules often limit the imagination and creativity of the artist, but here are some suggestions which will help insure good results:

1. Avoid sharp, angular edges or corners. They create strain and cracking. Clay adapts itself more readily to rounded edges and soft curves. Also, after firing, an edge that is too sharp can be dangerous—like a chipped glass, it is hard enough to lacerate the skin.

2. To add soft to harder clay in a project which cannot be completed in one sitting, slowly soften the hard clay with a damp cloth or sponge. Too rapid absorption of water by clay will cause cracks. Apply a coat of slip before adding new, soft clay.

3. To mend cracks on still-moist clay bodies, probe to the bottom of the crack and fill it with clay of the same consistency. Repeat if the crack reappears. Before allowing it to dry, a piece should be carefully inspected and all cracks repaired. If the clay is hard, the problem is much more difficult; more time and patience are required. First, moisten the area very slowly, probe to the bottom of the crack, and carefully fill it with a solution of slip or clay mixed with 50% by volume of grog.

4. Lightly sponge the surface of a piece, after it is shaped to completion, to remove rough and sharp edges. Do not, however, expect sponging to cover up poor work.

Slip (liquefied clay) is available in one-gallon containers, comes in many colors and varieties.

Dogs cast in white and red clay slip illustrate how initial clay color can be planned for effect.

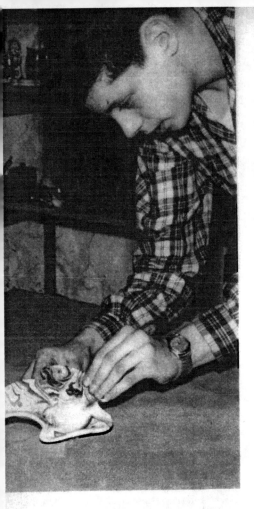

5. If a project is to be worked on over a long period of time, it must be kept damp between operations. A damp closet may be used. This is a specially constructed cupboard which is lined with zinc. An old icebox, a tin box or a butter tub with plaster cast across the top may also serve as storage vessels. The piece should be wrapped in a damp cloth, dampness depending on shape, size, sturdiness and condition of clay. Wrap the cloth *around* the object, to reduce weight on the clay, and *close* to the piece, to reduce evaporation.

6. Before a piece of sculpture is permitted to dry, it may need to be hollowed. If it is more than 1½ inches thick at any point, clay should be removed from the center. A half-inch wall of clay should be maintained. Hollowing allows the clay to dry with greater speed and with less stress and strain, and may open up air pockets which would cause disaster during the firing process.

7. How long a piece requires to dry depends entirely on its shape, thickness, and fragility. Slow drying under any circumstances is essential. Rapid drying causes a dry crust to develop on the surface, through which moisture cannot escape, and warping develops. Cracks may also appear at the points of greatest strain. A piece should be allowed to dry in its damp box until the shiny moisture disappears. Then it may be removed and left at room temperature for a day or so, after which it can be placed over a radiator or in a hot box where some means of heating is employed. Pieces must be completely dry before firing. Moisture turns to steam in the kiln and exerts tremendous pressure in escaping. This almost always results in the piece exploding.

To test dryness: In cold weather, place the bottom against the window pane for a few seconds. Look for condensation which will appear on the window if the piece is still too moist. There is no reliable dryness test for hot weather.

Finally, the novice ceramist should be familiar with a modeling material called plasteline, or plastecine. In essence, plasteline is comprised of ball clay, lanolin and glycerine. Since the clay flour is mixed with an oil base rather than water, plasteline is very plastic and will not dry, shrink or harden. It finds its greatest use for sculpting prototypes of castware. Unless the artist wishes to make reproductions of his sculpture, he should model directly in clay. Plasteline cannot be fired. A mold must be made of the plasteline figure and slip poured into it. When the mold is completed, the plasteline can be mashed up and used again. •

Marbleized effects shown below were very easy to produce. Objects are white with marbleizing of brown, red, blue, green, black, yellow, etc. To achieve them, just add powdered engobes in the desired color to your slip, prior to pouring it in the mold. Don't mix the color in; it will mix in itself as it pours, and with better results.

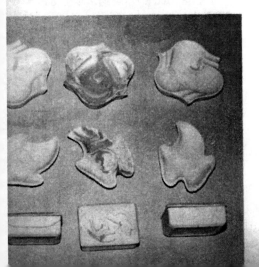

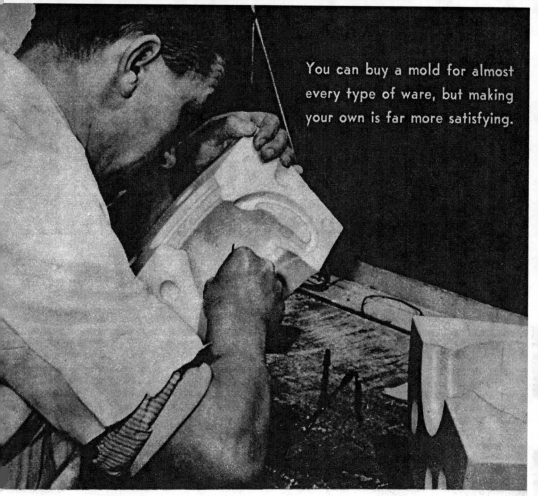

You can buy a mold for almost every type of ware, but making your own is far more satisfying.

molds—
how to make them

THE VAST majority of ceramic wares sold commercially today are cast in plaster molds. Only in expensive gift shops and art studios will you find original, one-of-a-kind, handmade pottery or sculpture for sale. Just as the assembly line makes it possible to manufacture automobiles in large quantity and at a popular price, so the mold makes it possible for the ceramist to produce multiple, inexpensive copies of a design.

There are all kinds of molds on the market today, which for the most part can be purchased by the hobbyist at reasonable cost. Most of these are more or less mass-produced by professional ceramists who

have created the original model. It is possible for you to buy a mold for virtually any type of ceramic ware you would like to turn out in your workshop.

However, you will find it surprisingly easy—and probably far more satisfying—to make your own molds, either of your own creations or of any other objects you feel would be worthwhile reproducing in clay. The model itself may be a ceramic piece; it may be made of plasticine, wood, glass or anything else. Remember, though, that a model made of thin and delicate glass is liable to crack when the plaster starts to set and becomes hot.

The simplest and most primitive type of

molds can be made from gourds, shells or baskets. Known as press-molds, these are capable of producing clay likenesses of themselves which can be imaginatively decorated. All you must do is powder the inside surface to prevent the clay from sticking, press in some plastic clay and smooth it with a damp cloth or sponge before it dries. When the clay has sufficiently hardened it can be shaken out gently.

Molds can also be made of clay which is fired at a low temperature so that the body remains porous. Such one-piece molds can be formed simply by impressing the model in them, or by working the clay around the model to the same shape. Such molds are capable of giving a sharper impression and finer detail than those made of plaster.

The most practical mold, however, is made of plaster. There are two ways molds are used. If plastic clay is used then you must have a press-mold. Generally speaking, however, molds are utilized for casting objects with slip. These are called pour-molds. Any press-mold can also be used for casting, and, in some instances, the reverse is true.

Let's assume you'd like to make a plaster mold of a water glass. Besides the glass you are using as the model, you'll need a small box, a brush, some liquid soap, a scraper and a medium-size bag of plaster. The box is used as a retaining wall for the plaster when it is poured and should be about one and one-half times as high as the model.

First step is to brush the outside surface and the top rim of the glass generously with the liquid soap. This procedure is called *sizing*. Now turn the model upside down in the bottom of the box. It is often a good idea to slide the glass back and forth a few times until a suction is created. It is necessary to size the item being molded in order to prevent the model from sticking to the plaster after it has set.

Mix a solution of potter's plaster and water to the consistency of thick cream. The more water you use the more porous your completed mold will be. Hence it will absorb more water and speed up the castings you will make in the finished mold. However, the mold will also be more fragile. Therefore it is better not to make your plaster mixture too liquid. One part water to two parts plaster is the rule of thumb.

Pour the plaster into the box. When it is full and the plaster has completely covered the glass, give the box a few smart raps. This will release any air bubbles which may have formed during the pouring. Once the plaster has started to set do not disturb it on any account, or it may not set at all. When the plaster has properly hardened, remove the box from around it. Turn the mold over and pick out the glass, which can be removed without difficulty because of the soap separator.

The final step in making any plaster mold is to *chamfer* the edges. This is the rounding off of all edges except those formed by the model. Take your scraper and trim off about one-fourth inch from the angles formed by any two outside faces of the mold. This is done so there will be no sharp angles or corners to break or chip.

You now have your first mold. Basically it is a casting mold, into which you will pour slip. (Instructions on how to use such a one-piece mold are given in the following chapter.)

Always store molds upon wooden sticks to permit air circulation around them; use them to stack.

Wedgwood with molded design is made by casting; many such shapes are easily made with molds.

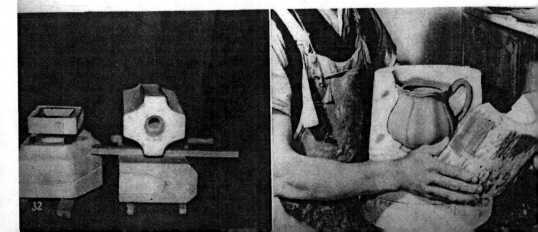

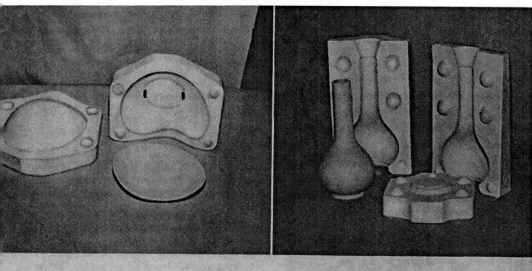

Above are a two-piece and a three-piece mold with the greenware cast from them—plate, flower vase.

If you had no trouble with this project, you can begin making many similar one-piece molds. For example, to make a simple press-mold, fill the box with plaster again and shake or vibrate to eliminate air bubbles. When the plaster has begun to set, but before it has become hard, push a button or ornament into it, making certain the back does not go below the surface of the plaster. Be sure also that the model has been liberally doused with liquid soap. When the plaster has set, you will have no difficulty removing the ornament.

Let the plaster dry for several days, then press a piece of plastic clay into the indentation left by the model, the same as you did with the aforementioned gourd- and shell-molds. Smooth the outside surface. Wait a few minutes for the plaster of the mold to absorb the moisture in the clay. This will cause the clay to shrink slightly, so that if you invert the mold and tap it gently, the clay reproduction will fall out.

A large variety of things can be cast in one-piece molds. However, a mold of two or more pieces is often required. The number of sections required in a mold depends entirely upon the number of *undercuts* in the model. An undercut is exactly what it sounds like—some part of the model which forms an angle that cannot be simply lifted out of a one-piece mold. The handle of a vase, for example, is a common undercut which must be cast in a two-piece mold. The separate sections of the mold can be individually removed, thus overcoming this obstacle.

In making your two-piece molds, let's assume you want to reproduce a milk pitcher.

Your first problem is to divide the pitcher-model into two equal parts vertically. This can be accomplished by drawing a thin dividing line along the outside vertical center. Dark watercolor paint and a fine brush are ideal for this. You may also use a thin glass-marking crayon. If a pencil is used, care must be exercised that you do not damage the surface of the pitcher with the sharp point. The line should bisect the handle as well as the main body of the pitcher.

Stop up the mouth of the vessel with a solid wad of clay, which should project two inches or so beyond the opening. This is called the *spare*. When the mold is made, the spare will cause a funnel-shaped opening at the top of the mold, through which you will pour the liquid slip with which you cast your ware.

The purpose of the spare is to insure that the top edge of the cast ware will be the same thickness as the rest of the piece, for slip settles into the mold as it dries and shrinks a little. If there were no spare to hold a small amount of extra slip at the beginning, the top edge of the model being cast would become irregular in shape and thinner than the rest of the body.

After you have completed the spare, imbed the pitcher in a block of soft clay up to the dividing line. Allow the spare, or clay stopper, to project slightly beyond the edge of this clay cradle. Smooth off the surface of the clay precisely level with the dividing line. If the clay bed falls below the centerline in places, build it up with surplus clay. Exactly half of the pitcher should be imbedded in the clay cradle; half should

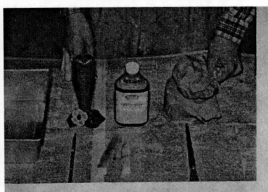

Left, to make your own mold start on flat surface spread with newspapers. For small item, a baking tin acts as form; otherwise make a wooden form. Items needed: tincture of green soap, brush, pencil, plastic clay, a wire-cutting tool, potter's plaster (to which you add water, 50% by weight).

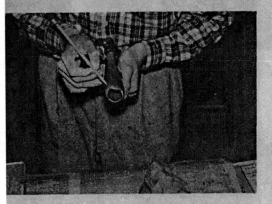

Below, mark even line around center of item to be molded. Fill half of the pan with plastic clay.

Imbed the item in clay up to the line you drew in the step above. Leave space around the master.

Fill top of vase with clay, making top contour rounded, and add spare (clay funnel for pouring).

protrude above the surface of the cradle.

Next you must build retaining, or restraining, walls around the block in which the pitcher is half-buried. The box-shaped form, of course, has no bottom or top. It should be at least two inches higher than the uppermost surface of the exposed half of the pitcher. You may construct the restraining walls of wood, linoleum, rubber or asphalt tile, or stiff cardboard. The smoother the walls, the smoother will be the exterior surfaces of the finished mold.

On your worktable now you should have a block of clay containing the half-imbedded pitcher, securely enclosed on four sides by the restraining walls, which should be tied or banded together. About an inch in, diagonally from each corner of the clay block, gouge out a semicircular hole. These four holes will be much like those a large marble would make if it had been pressed into the flat surface of the clay. Make each hole about three-fourths of an inch in diameter.

Using your liquid-soap separator, thoroughly cover the inside surfaces of the restraining walls. Then apply the soap generously to the pitcher itself. Prepare your plaster and pour to the very top of your wall form. When the plaster has set, you will have half of your two-piece mold.

Remove the walls and the clay bed from the model. Do not separate the pitcher from the plaster, nor remove the spare from the pitcher's mouth. Smooth all the plaster surfaces as much as possible, placing the mold so that the protruding portion of the pitcher is facing upward.

Construct four walls around the mold as you did before. The walls that were used for pouring the first section can conveniently be used again. Brush the *entire* top surface of the plaster with liquid soap, including the naked half of the pitcher. Many coats will be required on the plaster to make it sufficiently water-repellent.

The first section of the mold will have four raised hemispheres in the corners, where you gouged out the holes in the original clay block. When you pour in the plaster for the second section, indentations

After you've smoothed surface of clay evenly around vase, you are ready to paint interior and vase with green soap. This will prevent plaster from sticking. Now mix plaster slowly, as shown at right; too fast mixing will make air bubbles. Mold here is being made by author's son, George.

will be formed by each of these protrusions, forming a kind of lock that will hold both halves of the mold together securely and in the correct position when the ware is being cast. In other words, there is a male form and a female form with every two-piece mold.

After the second pouring has hardened, remove the walls. The right time to take the two sections of the mold apart is when the plaster has reached its maximum heat. Don't let the plaster get cold and then try to separate the sections. If you have difficulty, use a spatula or a dull round-ended knife and gently pry the sections free.

Remove the pitcher. Take away the spare. Chamfer all the outside edges of both pieces to reduce the danger of chipping. You should not attempt to cast anything in the new mold until it has had enough time to dry thoroughly. Several days is the minimum waiting period for the plaster to develop sufficient porosity to function properly.

Once you have mastered the technique of making one- and two-piece molds, there are literally thousands of ceramic items you will be able to cast in your workshop. For molding figurines, however, you will generally need a three- or four-piece mold. The extra sections are necessary to take care of the more complex shape.

Suppose you desired to make a mold of a squirrel figurine, sitting upright, its bushy tail behind. You may, if you wish, make individual molds of the squirrel's body and the squirrel's tail, cast them separately and then glue them together with slip before firing.

Or, you could make a single four-piece mold in which you can cast the entire figurine at one time. You will need one section for the front, and two for the back. In addition, another section should be made of the bottom of the squirrel so that the figurine-to-be will have a clay base. This is not absolutely necessary, but the base of the figure looks more finished if it is made of clay with a hole left near the center for casting purposes.

To make such a four-piece mold, the

Below, when plaster is of right consistency (a thick cream) pour slowly into pan, right to top.

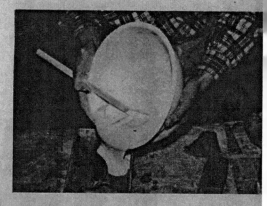

Now jog the baking pan, so that the mixture will level out evenly over the entire surface of pan.

When plaster is hard enough to remove from pan, you will feel heat in plaster; this is all right.

procedure is much like that for producing the pitcher mold described above. You begin by drawing the dividing lines on the model.

With the more complicated form of the squirrel, this will be a bit more difficult than it was with the pitcher. A simple way to find where the lines should be drawn is to look at the animal full face. The extreme edge of the silhouette is where you should draw the vertical lines on both sides of the squirrel's body.

Lay the animal on its stomach, so the lines are now horizontal. You can see why its tail necessitates your pouring two molds. One section over the tail could not be drawn loose. But if two sections are formed for the back, they could be drawn loose by pulling to each side. Thus, you must locate the vertical dividing line for the figurine's back and tail. This can be done by standing the squirrel sideways and looking directly at the silhouette of the profile. Again, the edge of the silhouette that you can barely see is where the line should be drawn. Begin at the highest point of the head, go directly down the back, up along the front of its tail, over the high point, and down the back of the tail.

When you have completed drawing the dividing lines, you are ready to make the first section of the mold. It's usually best to make the mold of the front of the figurine

Take half-mold you made and put clay strips all around. Gouge out two key notches for fitting.

Make another clay spare for top of vase. Tighten clay around. Next step is to soap vase as before.

Once again mix the plaster as you did the first time, add it to the vase for second half of mold.

When plaster has hardened, remove second half of mold from pan, and now you have complete mold.

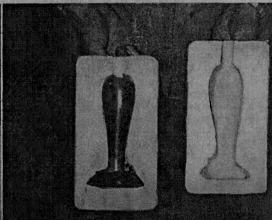

first, in order to reduce the chances of damaging the features.

Holding the squirrel with its face to the ceiling, build up around him to the dividing lines a cradle of soft clay. The clay surface should curve with the irregularities in the dividing lines along the animal's sides. The feet should be flush with the edge of the clay cradle, but there should be at least an inch to spare on the other three sides of the body. Now proceed as you did when you made your two-piece pitcher mold; build restraining walls, apply soap separator and pour the plaster. Do not, however, gouge out corner holes in the clay bed as you did before.

As soon as the plaster has set, remove the walls and the clay cradle. Smooth the surface of the plaster with sandpaper. With metal plaster tools, cut notches into the plaster wall on each side of the squirrel, which is still imbedded in the plaster. Because of the irregular shape of the model, some parts of the wall will be wider than others. Put your notches in the widest spaces.

Preparatory to making the second section, thoroughly brush the squirrel and the upper plaster surface with several coats of liquid soap. Place the animal on its side and build another soft clay cradle up to the dividing line drawn from the top of the head, down the back and over the tail.

Construct the restraining walls again to enclose this section and pour the plaster. As soon as it has set, remove the walls and the clay bed, but do not separate the model or the two sections of the mold. Smooth the new plaster surfaces with care and cut two notches in the new outside wall.

Apply several more coats of liquid soap,

especially to the newly formed plaster surfaces. Enclose the mold with restraining walls and pour the third section. When the plaster has set, remove the walls. Scrape the mold until it is neat and rectangular in shape. Turn the mold so the bottom side of the squirrel is up, and cut notches in two of the four walls.

You are now ready to make the fourth and final section. Cover the entire bottom surface of the plaster mold, as well as the base of the squirrel model, with ample brushings of liquid soap. It must be absolutely water-repellent.

Fashion a clay form in the shape of a funnel. Size, of course, depends upon how big the figurine is. If it's about five inches tall, then the funnel should be about two inches in diameter at the top and three-fourths inch diameter at the bottom. Place this over the center of the base of the squirrel to form the hole for casting. In the completed mold, this will be the hole into which you pour the slip.

Put up the restraining walls again and pour in the plaster. Remove the walls as soon as the plaster reaches its maximum heat. Then carefully open up the sections of the mold and remove the squirrel model. The notches you have cut in the plaster walls will fit together and serve as a key; each piece of the mold will fit only in its proper place when you start casting reproductions of the squirrel figurine.

Finally, chamfer the edges and dry thoroughly for several days before using the mold. With the know-how and practical experience you've gained in making these molds, you should be able to make all but the most complicated types of molds in your own workshop. •

Slipcasting mold and bowl made from it are shown below. To right of bowl is ash-tray drape mold.

Another type of mold is the press mold held in hand below. This is simple method of making tile.
Photos from "Craftsmanship in Clay"

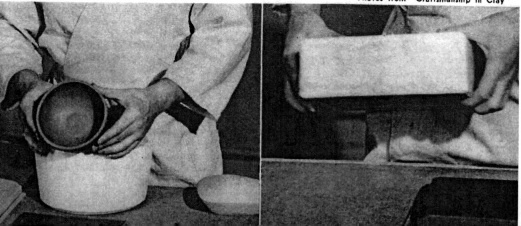

casting
and finishing

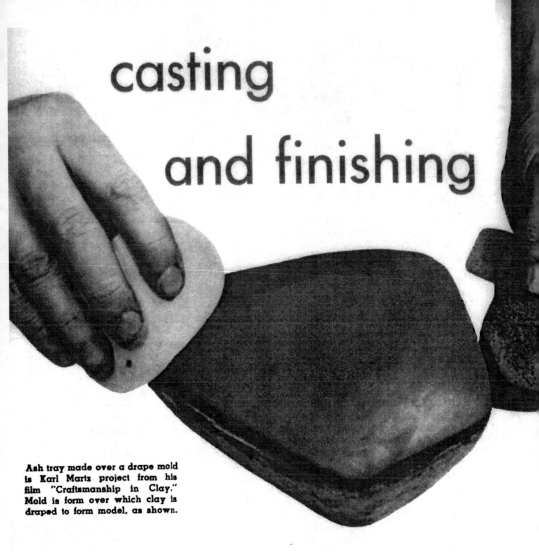

Ash tray made over a drape mold is Karl Martz project from his film "Craftsmanship in Clay." Mold is form over which clay is draped to form model, as shown.

Once you've mastered the individual problems inherent in various types of molds, take advantage of the time and money benefits of "mass production."

YOU ARE now ready to make your first slip casting. Let's begin with the simpler one-piece mold you made of the drinking glass. Remember, however, that before you use any mold you should make certain that it is absolutely dry.

The mold should be placed on a level surface, otherwise your casting will be lopsided. The slip container should be large enough to hold enough slip for the entire pouring. If you have to stop the flow of slip before the mold is full, there will be a scar on the ware where the pouring ceased. For this reason, you must never hesitate once you have started the pouring action.

After a few moments you will note that the slip which is in contact with the plaster wall of the mold is beginning to harden. Its color will begin to darken as the porous plaster absorbs water from the slip. The longer you leave the slip in the mold, the thicker this outside wall of drier clay becomes. Leave the slip in the mold until it has a wall at least one-eighth inch in thickness.

Then, very carefully, pour back the excess slip from your mold into your pitcher and place the mold upside down to drain.

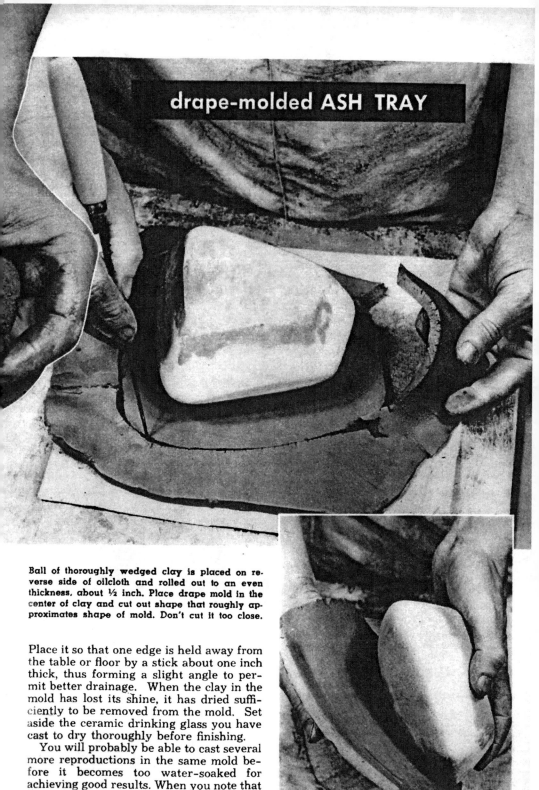

drape-molded ASH TRAY

Ball of thoroughly wedged clay is placed on reverse side of oilcloth and rolled out to an even thickness, about ½ inch. Place drape mold in the center of clay and cut out shape that roughly approximates shape of mold. Don't cut it too close.

Place it so that one edge is held away from the table or floor by a stick about one inch thick, thus forming a slight angle to permit better drainage. When the clay in the mold has lost its shine, it has dried sufficiently to be removed from the mold. Set aside the ceramic drinking glass you have cast to dry thoroughly before finishing.

You will probably be able to cast several more reproductions in the same mold before it becomes too water-soaked for achieving good results. When you note that the plaster is not absorbing moisture readily, put the mold aside to dry for sev-

Carefully fit the clay over the drape mold, and gently press down clay to follow shape and curve.

eral days. Then it will be ready to use again. You may hurry this drying process along by exposing the mold to warm air or an infrared lamp. Never try to bake it dry, however, since this is liable to deaden the plaster, making it incapable of absorbing water.

Casting in a mold of two pieces or more is not very much different than casting in a one-piece mold. Fit the mold together by matching the keys (the male and female hemispheres you formed in your two-piece mold, or the notches you carved in the multi-piece mold). Secure the pieces of the mold tightly together with rubber bands, such as those you cut from old inner tubes. If you have no rubber bands on hand, you may tie the pieces together with string. Simply cut notches on top and bottom edges of the mold to hold the string in place. Do not allow rubber bands or string to cover the hole into which you will pour the slip.

With a steady, even flow, pour the slip into the funnel-shaped opening, with the slip hitting the side of the opening and running down into the mold. The reason for this is that a hard spot is formed where the slip first comes in contact with the mold. This is caused by a concentration of salts.

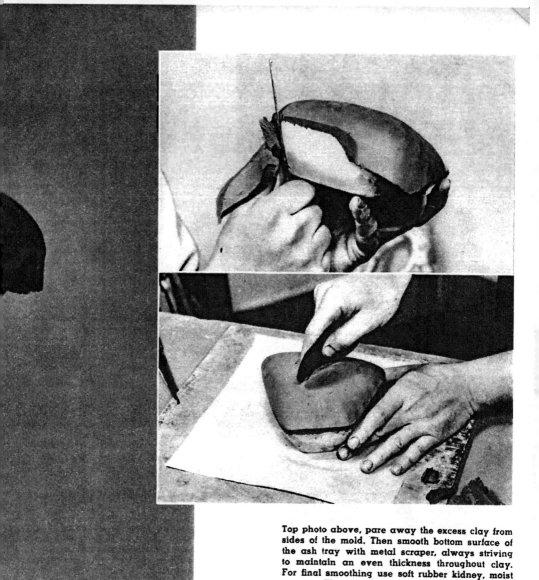

Top photo above, pare away the excess clay from sides of the mold. Then smooth bottom surface of the ash tray with metal scraper, always striving to maintain an even thickness throughout clay. For final smoothing use soft rubber kidney, moist sponge. Then, gently remove, dry, glaze, fire.

If this spot were on the surface of the piece, the glaze would not stick to it very well and a dry spot would result after the ware was fired.

Fill the mold to the top. The slip will sink in a few minutes as it settles and the water is absorbed by the plaster. Continue adding more slip until a wall about one-eighth inch thick forms at the top edge of the hole. Turn the mold over and pour out the excess slip. Remove the clay wall from the hole with a knife.

Wait for about twenty minutes to an hour for the clay to shrink away from the mold. Then carefully take the mold apart.

You should have a perfect reproduction of the original model. The slight ridges where the pieces of the mold meet can be scraped away when the piece is firm. This fettling process can be done with a sponge or brush within 15 minutes. It is safer, though, to let the piece become bone-dry before smoothing the mold marks away. Once the piece has dried completely you may fettle it with a knife and sandpaper or steel wool.

Many ceramists save all the dried slip they scrape from the pouring holes or collect from pieces which are damaged in the molding process. Such dried slip can be

ASH TRAY from a 1-piece mold

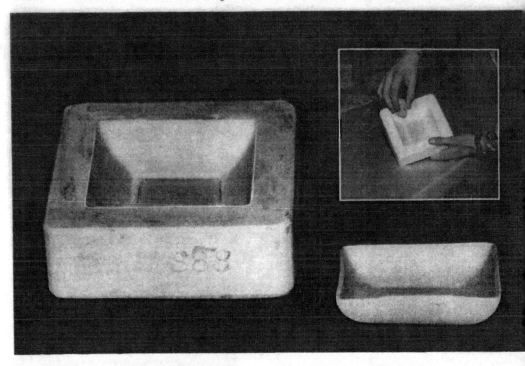

Above is one-piece mold and ash tray made from it. Remove dust from inside mold with dry sponge.

Left, slip is mixed thoroughly to creamy, smooth consistency. Mixing too hard may create bubbles in slip. One-piece mold is not easiest to pour since lip and edges require special care, but 16-year-old George Engel tries it for the first time. Below, he pours slip slowly into the mold; don't stop pouring or there will be mold marks on ware.

Allow the piece to drain on edge of stick, keeping the corner you used as a spout at the bottom.

Pour until the slip seems almost to overflow the edge, as seen above. The slip is actually higher. In about 10 minutes mold is ready for pour-out; blow softly on edge to check thickness. Let surplus slip drain back into jar, but don't let the mold be right-side up at any time while draining.

When ready, piece will come out when mold is reversed; it must be dry enough to maintain shape.

Three dogs above were made from same mold using different slips. Top dog is with red slip, glazed transparent; bottom dog is white slip. The dog at right is made from porcelain slip and is 10% smaller than others because higher firing vitrifies, shrinks it; it was glazed black and fired. Colored slips will temporarily stain your mold.

making a
CERAMIC DOG

Three heavy rubber bands are pulled in place to hold mold parts securely. Slip is then poured in one of the holes slowly and steadily. Slip will rise in all holes equally; when holes are filled add extra slip to each to make up for shrinkage.

Probably the most complicated mold you'll ever pour, this nine-piece one still isn't that difficult if you keep parts clean and dry, and assemble carefully. Top, parts are near where they assemble and are marked with indelible numbers for guide. Bottom, mold is assembled; the ninth part holds everything in place. Four pour holes receive slip and let out air as slip fills mold.

pulverized and used again by mixing it with a batch of regular slip. You should never use more than 10% of the reclaimed slip in any one batch.

There are several peculiar problems you are likely to encounter while casting with molds. A mold should be planned so that as shrinkage takes place in the slip, all areas shrink toward one central point. If a piece shrinks in different directions, the strain will cause it to crack and break in the mold. The form which best demonstrates this is that of an egg-cup. When such a shape is cast, the slip will shrink toward two points, one above and one below. The strain at the narrow neck in the center of the egg-cup would cause it to snap in two. For this reason, an egg-cup is best cast in two separate molds—one for the upper half and one for the lower half. The two sections are then stuck together with mending slip before firing.

Molds must also be designed so that no air can become entrapped when the slip is poured. If you were to cast an elephant figurine, for example, air would be caught at the tip of the trunk. The form of the animal would be upside down when the mold was ready for casting, and air would

44

Wait approximately 10 or 15 minutes—depending on how wet mold is from previous pourings—and pour out slip into receiving jar, again slowly and steadily. When most of slip is out turn mold upside down on two sticks to drain even further.

When the slip has dried enough to remove top of the mold easily, here is what you will see. This usually takes 10 to 15 minutes. If the mold is not ready to come apart, wait a little longer as forcing off top may damage piece you're molding.

be trapped in the trunk because it would have no way of escaping.

For models with similar dead-ends in the mold, carve a tiny vent into the mold with a knife which will permit the air to escape. A tiny stream of slip will run part of the way into the air vent when the cast is poured. This will break off when the clay cast is removed from the mold, and must be lifted out of the vent before the mold is used again.

Another special problem is presented when you cast an object with handles, such as a vase. If you cast the vase with handles and all, you must remove it from the mold as soon as the clay is strong enough to hold its shape—usually about 10 minutes after the slip has been poured. Otherwise, the handles are apt to snap off. This is a delicate procedure, since there is always the danger of distorting a piece by handling it so soon after it has been cast, while it is still in a semi-soft stage. For this reason, many ceramists prefer to cast vase and handles separately, the handles being stuck on later with slip. If any sections of the model are to be joined together—for example, handles on a vase or arms on a figurine—you should do so while the clay

is still damp. Use the mending slip on both surfaces to be joined and press firmly together. After a few minutes, remove the excess mending slip with a wooden tool and damp brush for the final smoothing.

Occasionally, very fine holes, called pinholes, will appear in cast pieces. Sometimes you will see them as soon as the ware is taken from the mold. Sometimes they will not show up until the piece is in the finishing process. Sometimes they will not appear until after the ware is fired.

Several things can cause these bothersome pinholes. If they appear on the mold side of the piece, it is more than likely that the mold was too wet when the slip was poured into it. If the holes show up on both the mold side and the inside of the ware, chances are they were caused by air trapped in the slip itself. Air can be trapped in slip if it is agitated too much, if it is strained carelessly, or if the clay in the slip is ground too fine. Pinholes will also mar the outside of a cast piece if the slip is poured too quickly into the mold. Dirt or other foreign matter in the slip, which burns out in the kiln, will cause pinholes to develop during the firing process. That's why you should always run

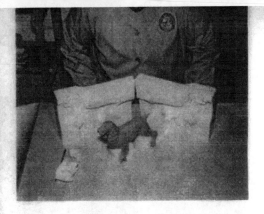

After you've opened mold, wait a minute or two and try to remove entire piece with plaster mold blocks still attached to legs. Then allow it to stand an additional three minutes on the blocks, and you will have a perfect piece of greenware.

Below, remove leg blocks and inspect for breaks and cracks. There shouldn't be any; if there are go over break with moist sponge. Then let dry on a plaster bat for about a week, until bone-dry. Bottom photo, ware has dried thoroughly and is gone over with fettling knife to remove the mold marks. Clean all appendages with utmost delicacy.

slip through a 40- to 60-mesh sieve before using it for casting.

In order to achieve peak results with any mold, it must be properly cared for. To mend a broken mold: First, the mold should be dry. Apply a liberal amount of orange shellac to the broken surfaces. Light with a match and allow to burn no longer than ten seconds, otherwise the heat will harm the mold. Extinguish the flame and press the broken pieces together, holding them firmly for approximately one minute. Any excess shellac that squeezes out should be cleaned off with a small tool and then wiped with a cloth dipped in alcohol. After drying for a day or two the pieces will stay firmly in place.

Too much stress cannot be placed on the necessity for keeping your molds spotlessly clean. Foreign matter or rough surfaces formed by caked slip will only ruin your castings. In cleaning a mold, use only a moist sponge. Any other method may damage the plaster.

Powder the inside of your mold with talc if it does not release cast ware easily. Sprinkle on a thin coat. The powder will show on the clay, but can easily be sponged off. Keep your molds in a dry place at room temperature. Dampness encourages fungi to grow on the plaster. By following these

When major cleaning-up is finished it is a good idea to go over areas where marks were with dry composition sponge, not rubbing too hard. Then use slightly dampened sponge, which will remove clay dust and provide good paint-holding surface.

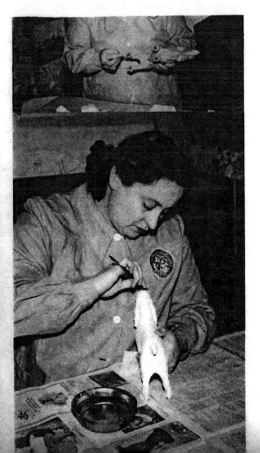

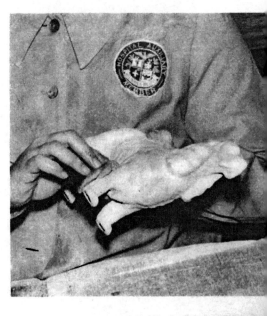

few simple rules, you will get many years of use from your molds.

Finishing

The pieces cast in your mold, after they are completely dried, are called greenware. Before this ware is decorated and glazed for the kiln, it must be smoothed, or finished. Unevenness, mold seams, fingerprints and other irregularities must be removed.

If a piece of greenware has been properly dried, this finishing process need not be difficult. Always strive for slow and uniform temperature when an object is removed from the kiln. A drafty, cold room might cause the ware to dry faster on one side than the other and make it warp or crack. The dangers of firing a piece which has not had all the moisture removed have already been discussed.

To finish a piece of greenware you will need one or more of the following: a fettling knife, a piece of fine sandpaper, a sponge, and a pan of water. Handle the piece with care. It is fragile and too much pressure might cause it to crumble in your hand.

First, you should fettle away the mold marks. As a mold gets older, the space between various sections of the mold be-comes larger, and the seams get correspondingly bigger. When the seams become too heavy, you should discard the old mold and make a new one if further casts of the piece are desired.

Never attempt to scrape the seams off a piece that is still damp—the knife marks will show through the glaze in the finished ware. Carefully take the dry greenware and hold the cutting edge of the fettling knife against the ridge left by the mold. Gently scrape it down until it is flush with the surface of the ware. Then carefully sand the seams with a fine sandpaper.

This will cause a clay dust to form on the surface. You can remove this dust with a damp sponge. Make certain that the sponge is not too moist. If it is difficult to sponge in some places—such as the inside of a small pitcher—you can use a stiff-bristled brush instead. If too much water is on the sponge or brush, it will wash away some of the clay, leaving the silica in the clay exposed. This is undesirable because the silica will make the surface of the ware rough.

The technique for mending cracks has already been discussed in the chapter on clays. To review briefly, dampen the area around the crack with a damp sponge. Probe to the bottom of the crack and fill with mending slip. •

It was decided to paint this piece as an English or Springer Spaniel, and this called for black on white. Do not be reluctant to go off beaten track in your painting; main thing is not to get duplication of live animal but a true "ceramic."

Piece is covered with transparent glaze, flowed on with uniform thickness. Flow glaze into leg openings to strengthen them. Dry-foot the ware. Inspect glaze for missed spots, easy to see as glaze dries. When piece is dry, place it in kiln.

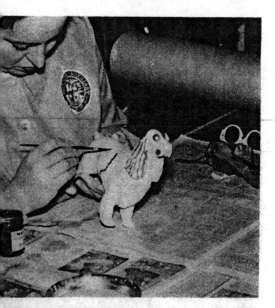

hand-modeling pottery

Once you've got the feel of clay you're ready to go a step beyond decorating and glazing, into more creative processes.

WORKING with castware, the ceramist's creative abilities are given free rein only in the decorating and glazing processes. If the mold has been purchased or made after someone else's original design, this is particularly true. Copying ideas may be excused at the beginning, when the tyro ceramist is more concerned with learning basic techniques than with producing prize-winning pieces. When these techniques are mastered, however, the clay worker should strive for originality. The sooner you decide to become a creative ceramist, the better. Imitating the work of others for too long will be a hindrance rather than a help in developing your own style of artistic craftsmanship.

In all probability, you will find handmodeling the fun part of your hobby. It is a supremely satisfying experience to dig your hands into a mass of good, plastic clay and fashion it into a pleasing, meaningful shape. Perhaps your first few tries at hand-modeling will not turn out the way you had hoped, but with practice you can eventually produce pieces that will satisfy you. And the knowledge that you created these pieces from masses of raw clay will let you taste the thrill which a sculptor such as Michaelangelo must have felt upon completing one of his superb masterpieces. When you have finished a piece which particularly pleases you, by all means make a mold of it if you wish. If others find the design as exciting as you do, then you might very well be able to sell reproductions of it.

Before attempting too ambitious a project, you must learn the fundamentals of forming an object with clay. Begin by wedging the clay until it has the consistency of putty. Repeat the wedging process several times, as described in the chapter How to Start. After several repetitions, the clay is wedged and pliable enough to work.

It is a good idea to get the feel of clay at the very start. This can be accomplished simply by taking a mass of clay and shaping it into a ball or ovoid about four inches in diameter. Then, with both hands, squeeze and press it into a simple form. Use no tools other than your hands. Slowly organize the clay ball into an abstract shape which is esthetically pleasing. This is an excellent way to begin pottery-making. As you shape the abstract sculpture, organize the clay into rhythmic shapes and stress those lines which seem the most pleasing.

After you have gotten the feel of the clay, you can begin making simple pottery. First, roll the wedged clay into a ball about two inches in diameter. Place the ball in your left palm and slowly press your right thumb into the center. Do the same with your left thumb until the bottom is about one-quarter inch in thickness. Keep both thumbs in the center, with your other fingers on the outside, and press out slowly, revolving the piece constantly.

Continue working the bowl until the entire wall is about one-quarter inch thick. When the piece is even in shape and

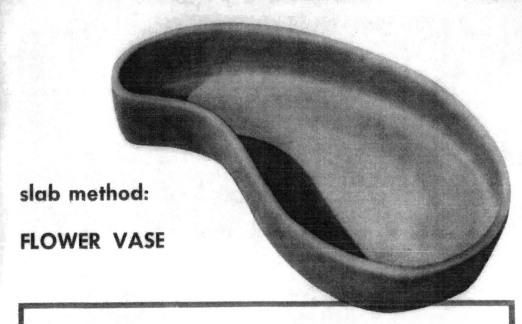

slab method:

FLOWER VASE

THE PROJECT *introduced above and the candlestick shown on a following page were planned and executed by Karl Martz, renowned author and teacher of ceramics technique at Indiana University's School of Fine Art. Mr. Martz's work has been purchased for many important public and private collections throughout the world. He was recently named "Outstanding Craftsman" by* House Beautiful *magazine; received the Maud Ainslie Craft Award from the Speed Museum in Louisville, Kentucky; was twice the winner of top honors at the National Ceramic Exhibition; and twice was awarded First Prize at the Indiana Biennnal Ceramic Exhibition.*

Formerly, Mr. Martz was a contributing editor to Ceramics Monthly *magazine, and is a charter professional member of the Midwest Designer-Craftsmen Association. The step-by-step photographs used to illustrate these two projects, as well as others used elsewhere in this book, have been taken from a series of films titled "Craftsmanship in Clay" which Mr. Martz directed for Indiana University.*

For the projects shown here, use any good plastic modeling clay. Directions will instruct you how to make the clay ware, which then must be finished, decorated, glazed and fired. If you don't want to invest in a kiln until you have experimented further in ceramics, check your local telephone directory to see if there is a school or commercial pottery in your vicinity where you can have your ware fired—at a cost of usually only a few cents a cubic inch.

thickness, you can easily model it further into an ash tray, small vase, demitasse, or liquor jigger. It can also be decorated in any manner you wish, and fired.

If you would like to make a larger vessel, roll a clay ball which is approximately seven inches in diameter. Cut the ball in two and allow both halves to rest on plaster bats. Scrape out the centers and work the walls with your fingers until they are between one-eighth and one-quarter inch

thick. Again, keep the pieces even in shape and thickness. When you are done, you will have two bowls, seven inches across and about three inches high. You may reshape these shells into any shape you desire, decorate and fire.

Another project which should give you no trouble at this stage of your clay-working skill is the making of a saucer. First, flatten a mass of wedged clay with your hand. Use a rolling pin to roll the

After rolling out clay, draw shape of the bottom of the vase as shown. Clay is about ½ inch thick.

Next, cut out the vase bottom with a sharp knife or special tool called a "prick." Pull clay free.

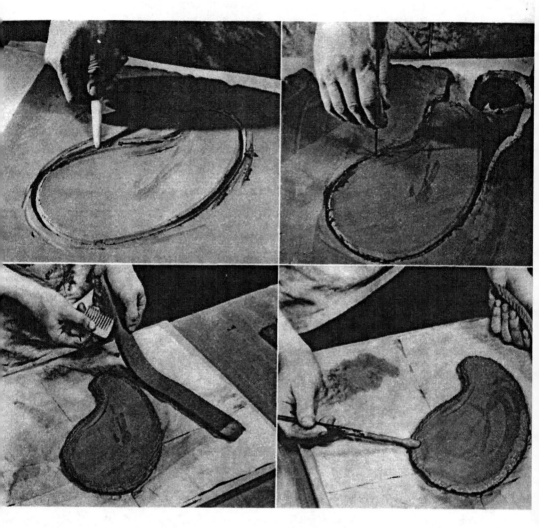

Cut long strip of clay, ½ inch thick, 2 inches across, long enough to fit half way around base.

Use comb to score strip and top edge of base, and coat rough edges generously with mending slip.

clay out to a thickness of one-eighth inch. Cut a circle about six inches in diameter. Smear some Vaseline on the bottom of an ordinary drinking glass, to prevent it from sticking to the clay, and place it in the center of the clay circle you have cut out.

Using the glass as a support for the clay circle, turn it upside down so that it rests on the mouth of the glass. You will note that the circle will droop at the edges. Finally, turn the newly formed saucer right

side up and remove the glass. Any additional shaping that is required can be accomplished by hand.

Now let's make something more ornate, yet not much more difficult—a leaf-shaped dish. Roll out your clay as before, lay a large oak or maple leaf on the flattened mass of clay. Cut around the leaf to form a clay leaf. With a toothpick, etch a network of veins on the leaf shape. Next, curl up the edges, supporting them with small wads of clay as the piece dries. When glazed and fired, you will have a handsome dish for your home.

There are many other everyday objects from which you will be able to gain inspiration for developing your own original forms. Easy-to-make flowers, for example, are useful as applique decorations when slip-glued to vases, bowls and other larger pieces. They can be simply produced by rolling about twenty pea-sized balls, flattening them, and using slip to join them together in petal shapes.

There are, of course, numberless objects which can be made with the basic techniques outlined so far. Once you have actually started working with clay, you will probably find yourself thinking constantly of new projects, many of which will be suggested naturally by the one on which you are working. You will, in fact, be limited only by your own ingenuity.

However, there are two other methods of construction which will open still wider vistas to the creative ceramist: the slab method and the coil method. Once you have mastered these, there will be virtually nothing you will not be able to make in the way of pottery, granting that you have at least a touch of talent. Neither of these much-used construction methods has changed since the earliest days of pottery-making, before the potter's wheel was discovered.

Slab Construction

Let's take the slab methods first. A good starting point is the making of a tile. Place a ball of wedged clay on your work surface. Lay two sticks of equal height on either side of the clay. With your rolling pin resting on the sticks, roll out the clay until it is a flat slab, exactly as high as the sticks. This will insure uniform thickness of the slab. Without your stick as a guide, your rolled clay would end up with one end thinner than the other.

If the clay shows a tendency to stick to your work surface or to the rolling pin, a sprinkling of talcum powder will absorb the excess moisture. Turn the clay over once during the rolling-out process to make sure both sides are smooth. Take away the sticks and cut out a 6x6-inch square with a sharp knife. This is your tile.

Leave the tile on a plaster bat until it becomes leather-hard. You must now scoop out the underside of the tile to prevent warping in drying and firing. You may cut squares or grooves half an inch apart, to a depth of one-eighth inch, or you can

scoop out a decorative pattern. Tiles should be dried slowly. After they are decorated and fired, they can be used for hot plates, table tops, trays, book ends, or any number of decorative purposes around the home. Be certain to true up the sides of your tile before putting it in the kiln. This can be done with sandpaper after the tile has dried, although some clays are better trimmed while still damp. Only experience can tell you when trimming is to be done.

Set the strip, or slab, in place on base, carefully fitting it at joint to the contour of base.

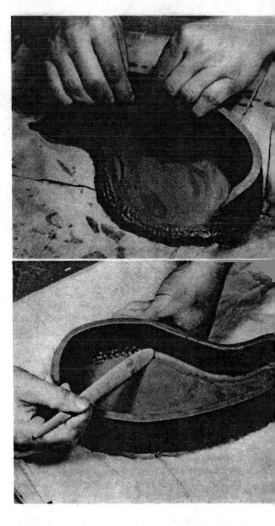

With vase wall complete, weld joints with wooden modeling tool, as before. This is important step.

You can see that by making five tiles and joining them together—four sides and a bottom—you can form a box. A sixth tile, laid across the top, turns it into a crude, square box with cover. This is the basic technique used in the slab method of construction. It consists primarily of constructing flat-sided pottery by joining together slabs of clay.

For your first slab-constructed project, let's make the box described in the pre-ceding paragraph. After you have cut six clay slabs, all equal in area and one-quarter inch in thickness, you should let them dry slightly before they are handled. In their plastic stage they will bend or warp too freely.

When the slabs have lost some of their plasticity, place one on your work surface to serve as the bottom of the box. Now erect the four vertical walls, using slip to join the contiguous surfaces. You will

After joining slab and base, knit the joint to-gether. Use a wooden modeling tool to do this.

Cut another slab to complete wall of vase, score edge, apply slip, and set in place in same manner.

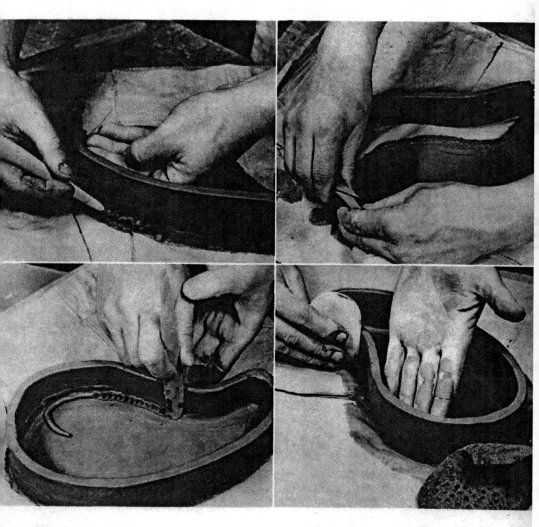

Now, to strengthen joints further, insert a thin coil of clay and knit it in place all way around.

Final shaping of sides of the vase is done with special modeling tool, rubber kidney, shown here.

have to trim two of the slabs to fit all four sides on the base. Reinforce all the joints by inserting coils of clay in the corners and, with a wooden tool, working the coils smoothly into the sides and bottom. If this is done skillfully, no traces will remain. Also weld the outside seams with finger or tool.

The sixth slab, or cover, should now be set in place. Check to see that it fits evenly. Trim off the excess if it is too large. A ridge or collar must now be put inside the cover so that it will not slip off the box. Put a pellet of clay at each of the four corners of the underside of the cover, but in front of the edge to allow for the thickness of the sides of the box. Measure the distance in from the edge before placing the pellets. Put the cover back on the box. The fit should be snug, without any play. If the cover does not fit properly, move the pellets until it is held firmly in place.

Below, a metal scraper is employed to smooth the bottom of vase for a fine, finished appearance.

Edges of sides are beveled with wire tool. This is done to prevent chipping of edges in future.

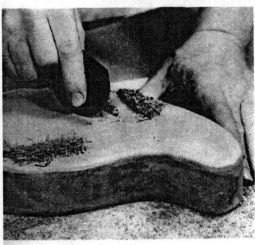

Turn vase over and again use metal scraper to apply smooth bottom surface. Practice using tools.

Erase tool marks with damp sponge, handling carefully—no fingerprints! Now proceed to decorate.

cutaway slab:

CANDLESTICK

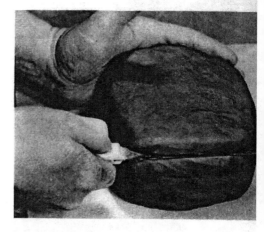

Start with ball of damp, wedged clay and press it into rectangular shape; cut ¾-inch slab at top.

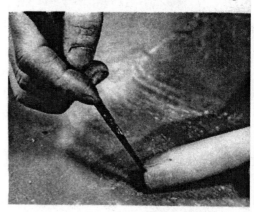

Take candle and notch its base to prevent its sticking to clay; below, it forms hole in clay.

Score a path about one-quarter inch wide between the pellets, paint it with slip, and weld a small coil, one-quarter inch thick, all around. Smooth to a square ridge with tools. The box is now complete and ready to be decorated.

Constructing this simple box has certainly opened your eyes to the many other objects you will be able to make by the slab method. Any manner of flat-sided ceramic pieces can be made just as handily: ash trays, cigarette boxes, vases, cheese dishes, etc. The shapes need not be square. Matter of fact, the square is generally considered to be rather a dull proportion, esthetically speaking. The rectangle is far more interesting to the eye. When you begin making other slab-con-

Press candle into center to form candlestick pit. Original ball of clay was 8 inches in diameter.

structed items, you may find it helpful to use paper patterns as a guide for cutting out the clay pieces to insure correct size and fit.

Curved or round forms can also be constructed with slabs, but it is advisable to make such forms by the coil method because it is a freer method and the results will probably look less mechanical. If slab construction is used to make these forms, the process is similar to that for making flat-sided objects. The only difference is that the bottom is circular or organic in shape and the slab for the side is made of one continuous piece and fitted to conform with the curve of the bottom. As with flat-sided pieces, the sides may be vertical or made to taper or flare as desired.

Coil Construction

The coil method of construction is best understood by building a simple bowl. The

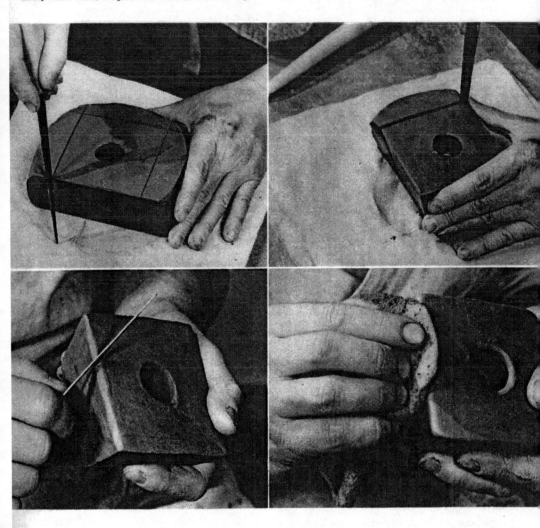

word "build" is used advisably, for that is exactly what you do when you use the coil method—build up an object by placing clay coils on top of one another.

The bowl base may be made with a round slab, three-eighths inch in thickness and two inches in diameter. Place this circular slab on a plaster bat. Then, on a piece of oilcloth placed downside up on your work-table, roll a piece of clay with your hands into a long even coil, long enough to fit

Compare rough-cut candlestick with one below it. Finishing touches will be added: note side angle.

Above, the finished candlestick, ready to be decorated, dried, glazed and fired—and then used.

around the circumference of the base. The coil should be a little thicker than the walls of the bowl are to be. Cut the ends of the coil on the diagonal and weave them together to form a complete circle. The ends may be joined with slip, too. But make certain they are cut on the bias before joining them. This prevents lumps at the point of juncture and also presents a larger surface for adhesion. Work the coil into the base with a wood tool or your thumb. Start about halfway up the coil and draw the clay gently but firmly into the base. So long as the clay is soft and pliable it is easy to weld. Continue building up the walls of the bowl by placing coil upon coil, making each succeeding coil a larger circle.

You can, if you wish, form the base with a coil instead of a slab. This is done by holding down one end of the coil firmly to your work surface while winding the balance of the coil in concentric circles around the end you are holding in position. Should cracks appear in the winding it indicates the clay was not properly wedged or that it is too dry. When the coil base is finished, you will have a hook-rug effect. Now you can attach the next coil, the same as you did to the slab base. Continue building up coil layers, joining each on top and bottom with slip.

Make your bowl about three inches high, with a diameter across the top of approximately four inches. As you attain more skill, you will be able to start with a coil base and continue winding right up to the top of the bowl, adding new coil lengths as they are needed, using slip the way a builder uses mortar.

If you are constructing a large piece, it may be necessary to halt about halfway up the wall and allow the clay to dry slightly, to a leathery consistency, in order to give it sufficient strength to support the weight of additional coils. In such a case, you should thoroughly moisten the point at which you commence your next step of the project. Otherwise the leather-hard clay will not adhere readily to the damper new clay coil. This may be done by placing a moist cloth on the top coil.

When constructing a symmetrical piece, say a vase or pitcher, it is generally advisable first to cut out a cardboard template. This will permit you to make periodic checks on the symmetry of the piece as you go along.

As you work, you should add a little water to your fingertips occasionally. It is very tempting to use too much water be-

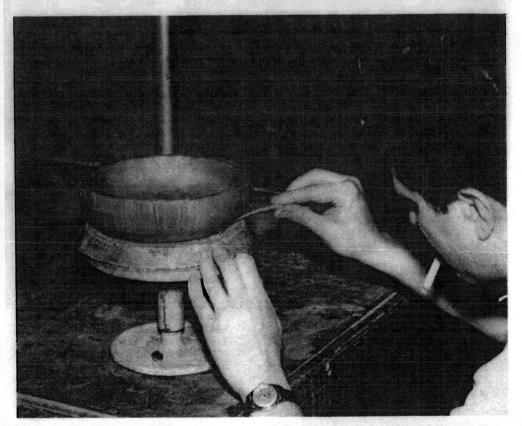

coil method:

DECORATIVE BOWL

Domenick Angelo of Sculptors and Ceramic Workshop smooths outside of bowl made by coil method. When surface is even it can be textured with a rough-edge stick or saw blade. For very smooth finish go over lightly with elephant-ear sponge.

cause water smooths the clay so easily. But do not get the clay too moist, or the vessel may collapse.

Many ceramists prefer to remove the surface ridges which are formed by the coils. This can be accomplished by filling the valleys with slip or soft plastic clay and smoothing with the fingers to erase the curvature of the coils and fill in the seams between. Rub the model with the back of a spoon if you want a very smooth surface.

Cracks are a virtual certainty during the drying period if the coils have been welded improperly. These cracks can be mended, but this is an unnecessary bother if the vase had been constructed carefully originally. Add water around the crack until the clay is once again plastic. Gently cut and lift out the cracked section of the coil.

Then fill with a fresh coil, gently working in the new clay to meld with the surface.

When the piece has dried it can be sanded smooth. If, however, you desire the coil marks to remain on the finished ware, sand away only the slip marks where the coil ends were welded together.

Spouts, Covers and Handles

Many of the wares you construct by either the slab or coil method will require spouts, cover and handles. For example, there are such things as pitchers, teapots, sugar bowls and cookie jars, to name but a few.

Two types of spouts—the triangular and the tapering tubular spout—serve all purposes. After the main body of the piece is formed, mark the place where the spout is to go and cut out a round or triangular

Take regular plastic clay and roll it to thickness of ¾ inch. Place clay between two sticks of this thickness for easy way to roll it evenly.

Using lid from a canning or fruit jar as a cutting mold, punch out the base for bowl from the clay. Upon this base you will start first coil.

Here is punched-out slab base. Coil base can be used for this type of project, too. Work on plaster bat, and cover table with reversed oilcloth.

Next, roll out the coils of clay for constructing the sides of the bowl. Keep the rolls even, and not too large; clay used should be soft, pliable.

Using a clay modeling tool, roughen up the edges of your base and apply a thin layer of slip (liquefied clay) onto the roughened clay edges.

Work first coil around your base firmly by applying pressure with thumb, forefinger. You will feel slip take hold of coil, like layer of cement.

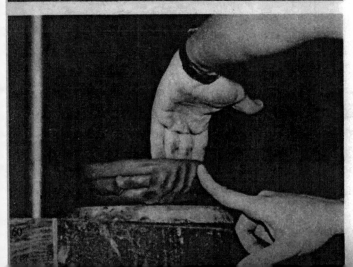

Continue adding coils, one on top of another. Add slip between each layer of coils, to unite them firmly. Do this until reaching desired height.

hole, depending upon which spout you want to use. Both types of spouts are fashioned with coils.

To make a triangular spout, join the ends of each coil to the model and weld them in place. Each coil is larger than the one beneath it. Also weld the coils inside and out. When you are done, you should have an inverted, three-sided pyramid, the V-shaped coils forming two walls and the main body of the ware forming the third side. Be sure to score the model and paint it with slip as you weld the coils to it.

If the spout is tubular, and tapered and curved, make circular coils and weld the first to the model around the outer edge of the hole. Score the joint and paint it with slip. Add a second coil to the first, and so on, making each coil a smaller circle to form the taper, and adjusting it to the desired curve. Weld each coil to the preceding one as you work.

Covers may be made in two ways. They can be fashioned separately and fitted like the one you made for the slab-constructed box. Or they can be made as part of the object and cut away. The latter may be the better way when making a round or symmetrical piece because it insures a more perfect fit. Continue building your ware, say a teapot, with coils until you close the top. Then mark off the cover and cut on the scored line with a sharp knife. Lift off the cover. Add a coil and form it into a collar so that the lid will not slip off the pot. Also join a projection to the bottom side of the collar to keep the lid from dropping off when the pot is tilted.

A handle for the cover can be made in a number of ways—a flat knob, a ball, a hemisphere, or a loop. Glue it to the cover with mending slip.

The larger handles for the sides of the ware itself are made in much the same way. Most used for this purpose, however, are loop handles. Such a handle can be made of a clay coil, round or flattened. Make certain the handle is sturdy enough. Keep it in proportion to the size of the piece. Likewise, the shape of the handle should be suitable to the shape of the object for which it is designed. A heavy beer mug, as an illustration, would look ridiculous with a tiny delicate handle originally intended for a demitasse cup.

Join the handle to the main body of the ware by scoring the points of contact and painting with slip. Clean off the excess slip and smooth the juncture with a sponge while the piece is still moist, or a fettling knife and sandpaper after it has dried. ●

[*Turn page for additional photos*]

how to make a
SMALL TILE

Tiles can be used in table top, for a fireplace facing, etc. Here, Gertrude Engel demonstrates method of making one, using regular plastic clay.

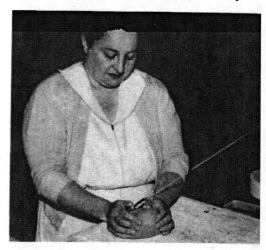

Wedge clay until plastic, slice under wire and check for air pockets; if none, you can begin. To counteract shrinkage, start with clay 15% larger.

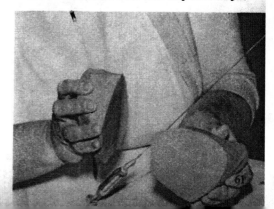

Place ball of clay on reversed piece of oilcloth and center it between two ¾-inch high sticks.

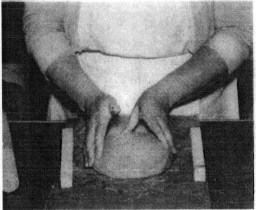

Use a rolling pin to level and spread the clay. If roller sticks, powder it lightly with talcum.

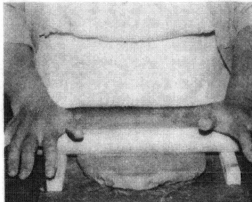

Measure out your clay size. For this tile, 6-inch square was wanted, so marks of 7 inches are made.

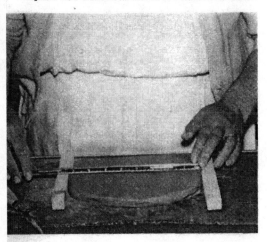

With ruler and kitchen knife, cut out the square. Cut the clay with downward motion at the corners.

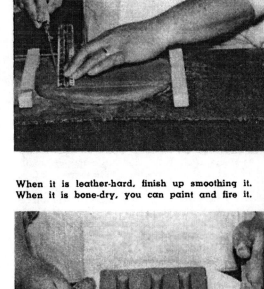

Use wire tool to gouge out several panels in the back to prevent kiln warpage; dry on plaster bat.

When it is leather-hard, finish up smoothing it. When it is bone-dry, you can paint and fire it.

Courtesy The Metropolitan Museum of Art

English hand-modeled chess set has white ceramic clay bodies
with decorative underglaze colors and transparent overglaze.

Ash tray of white clay body overlaid with an interesting
glaze pattern and engobes has texture worked into background through use of small wire brush with a 90° angle.

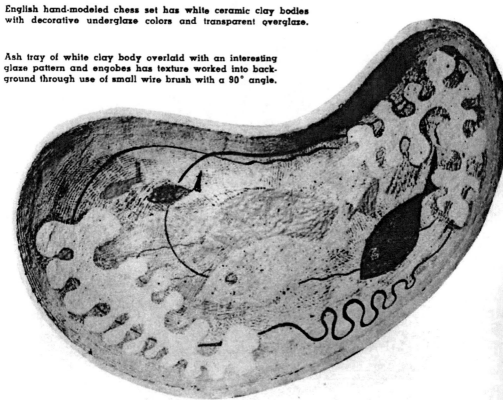

Sculptors and Ceramic Workshop photo

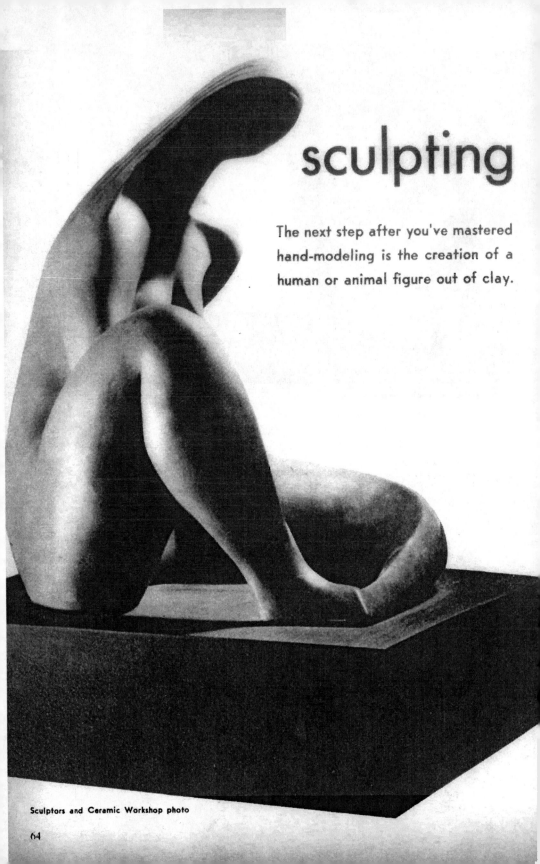

sculpting

The next step after you've mastered hand-modeling is the creation of a human or animal figure out of clay.

hollow-constructed
HARLEQUIN

THE TECHNIQUES you learned in the preceding chapter for hand-modeling pottery will stand you in good stead when you begin sculpting figures. While it is not sculpture in the purest sense of the word, you can create simple animal shapes by taking a handful of wedged sculpture clay and pressing it into an abstract form—the same as you did to get the feel of clay before making your first piece of pottery.

The abstract itself should suggest a realistic shape to you. If not, continue twisting and pressing the clay mass until it does. Then follow out the suggestion by modeling further with fingers first and then with tools if you desire. A good rule to follow when sculpting is to disregard all but the most essential detail. As often as not, slavish accuracy detracts from the beauty of a ceramic piece rather than adding to it. It is sound procedure to make a sketch of your model before working it in clay, striving always to keep the lines uncluttered and clean. Keep your shapes as simple and basic as possible.

When sculpting a figure, its size will have a direct bearing on the type of clay you should use. Obviously, when modeling a large figure, the clay must be both plastic enough to shape and at the same time strong enough to hold up under its own weight. This is a minor consideration in the sculpting of smaller pieces since there will not be too much stress or weight involved.

Sculpting clays which are commercially prepared generally contain reinforcement ingredients to prevent cracking, warping, and to reduce the likelihood of a cave-in. Grog is the principal material added to clay for this purpose. (See the chapter on Clays.)

Coarseness of the grog depends upon the size of the figure-to-be. The larger the figure, the coarser must be the grog. The amount of grog used will also increase in a direct proportion to the size of the intended sculpture. As much as 50% of the clay body must be comprised of grog in an exceptionally large piece.

Before mixing grog with clay, you must first ascertain how much clay will be used to make the model. This is done by dividing the clay into sections which are small

To make harlequin above, a hollow shape is constructed by pinch method of adding small pieces continuously to make a wall about 1 inch thick.

Shape below is in rough-ready stage and ready for shaping. Sculptor is Anne Hossack from Canada, student at Sculptors and Ceramic Workshop, N. Y.

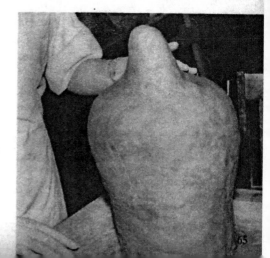

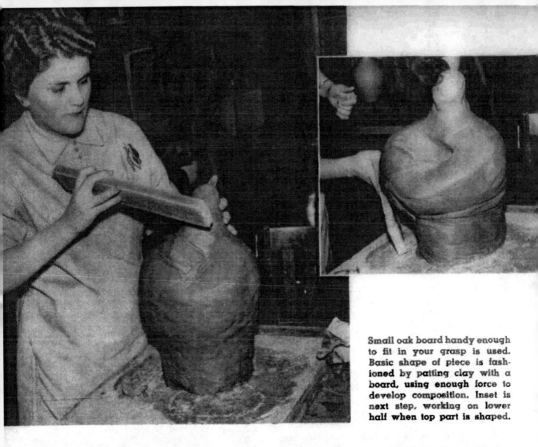

Small oak board handy enough to fit in your grasp is used. Basic shape of piece is fashioned by patting clay with a board, using enough force to develop composition. Inset is next step, working on lower half when top part is shaped.

enough to be individually wedged. Each section is weighed. Then weigh out the proportionate amount of grog for each section. This will probably range between 15% and 50% by weight. The larger the figure the more grog must be added.

Roll out each section of clay separately and scatter the proper amount of grog over the surface. Fold the flattened clay in half, then in quarters. Roll it out again. Continue folding and rolling until the grog is distributed evenly throughout each clay section, then wedge each thoroughly.

There are several methods for sculpting a figure of solid clay. Which you use will depend a great deal upon size, shape and the fragility of the piece.

For your first sculpting project, you may hand-model a human figure about five inches tall. Begin by determining the general outline with a pencil sketch. Simplify the drawing as much as possible, dividing the figure into its most prominent and least prominent parts. The most prominent part of a peasant woman, for instance, would be her wide, billowing skirt. Second in prominence would be her torso, which includes two arms, a short neck and a small round head. With your pencil, draw a horizontal line at the waist, another at the neck and

one more at the top of the head. If the figure is drawn to the same size as it will be modeled in clay, these lines will give you the three basic proportions of the piece.

A figure such as this will need no base, since the wide skirt can serve as a support for the model. Use clay that is very plastic, so that it can be worked easily and joined together without slip. Take a mass of clay and work it into the general shape of the peasant skirt. Do the same with the torso and attach it atop the skirt. Cut the length of a coil in two and attach one half to each side of the torso at the shoulders, to form arms. Keep them close to the body rather than having them stick out in space. Now attach an egg-shaped ball of clay for the head.

At this point you should have a crude representation of the peasant figure. It will be a bit larger than the finished sculpture will be, since you now have to carve off some clay to form a more detailed figure. Remember also that the model will shrink a bit as it dries.

Outline the skirt with a wire tool or wood modeling tool, whichever you find easier to work with. Keep turning the figure at regular intervals as you sculpt in order to get the proper three-dimensional perspec-

To form bottom half of sculpture, Anne Hossack uses similar procedure. Hollow ball is built for abdomen and two hollow cones shaped for the legs.

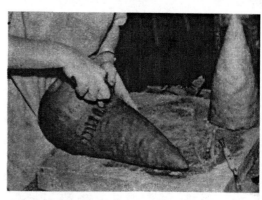

Now the leg or shaped cone is added to abdomen or ball. The joints are worked together with slip, and then knitted together by use of the fingers.

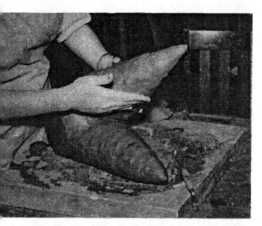

Other leg is added to the abdomen next. Again, slip is used for joining. When knitting joints together, work the thumb and forefinger together.

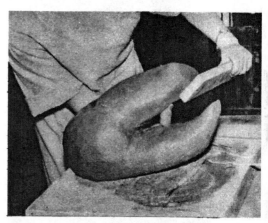

Oak board is used again to fashion the legs, and shape is made to correspond in harmony with the upper part of structure; planning is important.

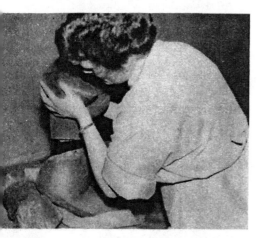

Hexagonal hole is made in lower half, so that upper half can be fitted in. This is called Roman Joint, will hold two pieces secure after firing.

Here is how the two pieces look when they're fitted together for the first time. Keep spraying device handy to sprinkle water if piece dries too fast.

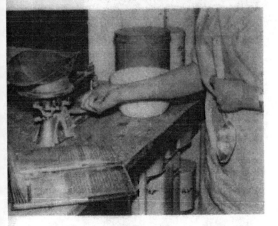

Ready for decoration: engobes (colored slip) will be made now. Ingredients are weighed, placed in a mortar and pestle and then ground thoroughly.

Recipe (ratio of parts): china clay 25; ball clay 20; ground flint 30; feldspar 17; whiting 2; magnesium carbonate 6. Weigh out parts accurately.

Engobe has been mixed and now is scrubbed into piece thoroughly with soft bristle brush called mottler. Design will be scratched through engobe.

tive by viewing it from all angles. Gouge out valleys and rounded ridges to form the folds of the skirt. Keep these at a minimum, just enough to suggest a piece of cloth which hangs freely from the hips.

When you have finished the skirt to your own satisfaction, start to work on the torso. Score the figure along the line where the arms are held against the body. Don't bother with the fingers. Such minute detail is superfluous. Merely form the suggestion of a hand. The bosom should be represented by outlining a gentle curve.

Do not be too concerned with the facial features, which will probably be painted in before firing. Just the slightest indication of nose, lips and eyes is all that is desirable. By placing a head scarf on the figure, you will not have to be bothered with defining the ears or hair. One final touch may be the shoes protruding a bit from beneath the skirt.

Chances are that you won't be able to complete the figure in one sitting. If this is the case, place a damp cloth over the partially finished work to keep it moist and plastic. The best place to store it between work periods is in a damp box or under a crock. After it has dried to its leather-hard stage, use a small spoon or a knife to hollow it out. Maintain a wall thickness of at least a half inch.

This hollowing process can be eliminated if you wish by starting your original crude form around a wad of newspaper. There is no difference in the sculpting procedure, and when the figure is placed in the kiln for firing, the paper will burn away, automatically leaving the figure hollow.

After you have completed this first piece of sculpture, there is a wide diversity of subject matter and treatment available to

Scratch in design, add color for additional interest. Piece must dry before it's kiln-fired; any moisture left in the piece will make it explode during firing.

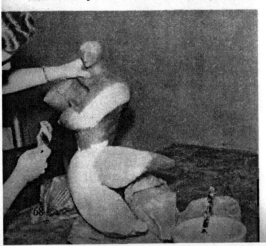

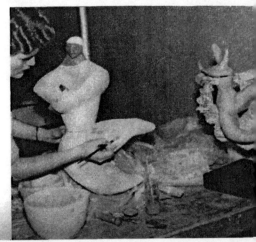

slab-built
HORSE

Clay body containing 3% iron oxide is to be cleaved, sliced on wedging board into small squares ½ to ¾ inch thick and about 4 inches square. This is first step toward making horse shown in photo above.

Grog is sprinkled liberally on each piece and distributed so that there's an even amount on each. Hollow-slab construction method is demonstrated here by Domenick Angelo, student at Sculptors and Ceramic Workshop, who just returned from Rome after using benefits of scholarship he won from Boston Museum School of Fine Arts.

Clay squares are then stacked up, just like so many sandwiches, one on top of another. You can prepare quite a bit of the clay in one operation.

The clay must be wedged, by slamming it down on the wedging board hard. Purpose of this is to mix clay evenly with grog; continue until it is.

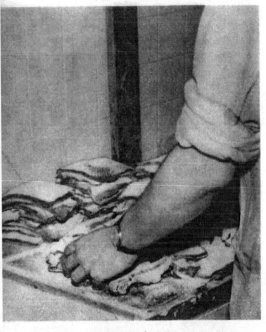

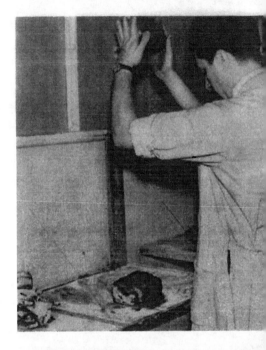

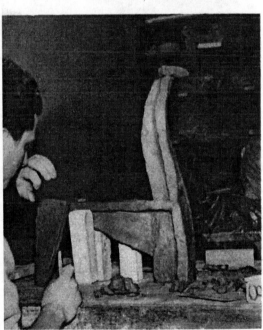

Slabs are allowed to become firm, light leatherhard, so they will maintain position when placed. You can support them with wood or ceramic blocks.

Advantage of working in this manner is that you can always change position of appendages. Other slabs are added to maintain stability of design.

Sprinkle a large board lightly with ground flint to cover surface. Then slice clay to approximate size and width for proper development of design.

Here slabs are covered over basic clay structure to enclose the skeletal form; slices are around ½ inch thick. Note that head position is altered.

you in your workshop. By following these same steps, you can produce portrait busts, whimsical or realistic animals and all manner of human figures.

There are limitations to this type of sculpture. For one thing, it is usually difficult for the amateur to construct large pieces by this method. And for another, it is extremely risky when you are making figures with large unsupported areas, such as the body of a horse or a dachshund. Moreover, it is not a practical method for sculpting figures with fragile arms and legs which protrude from the body rather than hug it as part of the main mass.

In cases where the figure is to have thin legs, for example, it is helpful to work with an armature, or a skeleton structure of the desired form. An armature can be made of wood, papier-maché, wire or a combination of these materials. Its main purpose is to support the clay form while it is being modeled. It is also handy as a guide for the sculptor who has trouble reproducing objects in clay.

Shape the armature to form the skeleton of the model. Then build up the clay around this skeleton, always keeping the ultimate shape in mind. When you have modeled the general contours of the figure, add smaller pieces of plastic clay and work them into the figure with a wooden tool to get the desired effect.

A wire armature should be removed before the piece is fired. If it cannot be removed, the piece should not be fired. For this reason, the wire skeleton is most often used with plasteline instead of clay and a mold made of the finished piece for casting reproductions.

When working with a wire armature, be sure to cover the entire skeleton. If a piece of the armature shows after the figure is well along, it is almost a disaster, for the armature is difficult to bend so that it won't show—and cutting it away would weaken the whole structure of the figure.

If you are constructing a figure from which the armature will not be removable after the figure is completed, you are better off using a wood or papier-maché skeleton. Unlike the wire armature, a portion of these should be left exposed so the skeleton will burn away in the bisque firing.

You can also construct sculptured forms by the coil method. For smaller pieces, you may use the coils as "sticks"—that is, you can sculpt in much the same way a kindergarten child draws a stick figure. To make a horse, for example, use a coil for the animal's body, four thinner coils for

Modeling of the horse is now complete. Piece is now ready for surface designs, which can be varied according to personal preference of worker.

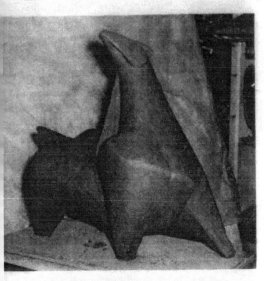

Tines of kitchen fork were used to develop continuous series of lines that conform to surfaces.

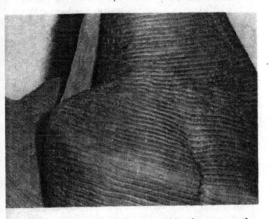

When finished piece is throughly dry, it can be fired in kiln; if you wish, ornament it further.

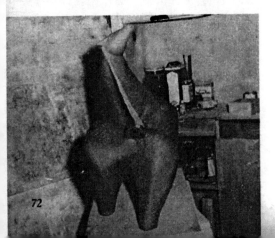

Expressive, deep eyes and gaunt, high cheekbones are especially suited to a technique like this. Appeal is lasting.

its legs. Add a coil for the neck and one each for the head and the tail. Make the coils thick or thin, long or short, as needed, but make sure they are sturdy enough to support any weight they must bear. Add clay where it is needed and shape the horse accordingly. Now apply the finishing touches, smoothing the surface, scoring the back of the neck to suggest a mane, indicating the facial features, etc. Always work with clay that is well wedged and plastic.

For larger pieces, this method is not practical. But larger pieces can be sculptured from outlines or forms built up by coil construction. To make a sitting owl, for example, build up the body shape in the same way you would construct a vase by the coil method. Add the coils in wider and narrower circles as necessary, until the hollow body shell is formed. Continue adding coils for the head. Smooth off the ridges formed by the coils. Indicate the bird's wing by scoring lines on each side of the body. Weld on two pointed ears at the proper places on the head. You can form the eye impressions and the beak by pinching the front of the owl's head.

Bull is interesting study of ceramic and metal composition; horns, tail are metal, cast after piece was made and fired. Small rolls or dabs of clay provided boy's facial texture.

If you wish, you may go further and suggest the texture of feathers on the body. However, an overdose of detail is generally not worth the trouble. Moreover, the longer you work on the sculpture the more risk you run of accidentally damaging it. With a project such as this it is advisable to work from a sketch or a photograph of a real owl. When the piece is completed, cut a hole in the base before firing. Since the body is already hollow, you will not have to worry about scooping clay from the center or removing an armature.

Sculpture can also be accomplished by a method which could be called the slap-dab method. This type of construction calls for consummate skill and can be too ambitious a project for the untutored and inexperienced clay worker. The outline or form is built up with masses of clay, dabbed in place and worked into the model by hand, using a very plastic clay. The piece is not built as a solid figure, later to be hollowed. Rather, it is constructed much the same as by the coil method. The figure is shaped with thick walls, and is hollow. Then it is sculpted to completion. •

the potter's wheel

Throwing and turning ware are fascinating techniques and look easy, but they're deceptive. The potter's craft requires lots of practice.

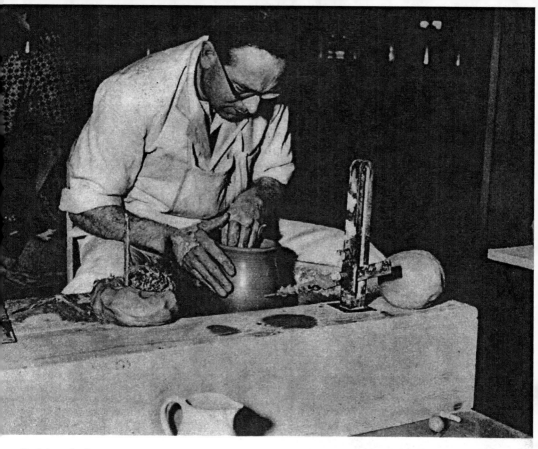

At left and above, practiced professional craftsmen turn out famed Wedgwood ware in Great Britain.

MUCH of the glamour of the potter's craft is associated with the wheel. Undoubtedly, the making of a model by throwing and turning on a wheel is the most fascinating of methods for making pottery. Faster, more precise methods have replaced the wheel in the modern commercial ceramics factory, but the ancient tool has remained as an important implement for the artist-potter.

Throwing is the technique of building a ware with the aid of the spinning of the wheel. *Turning* refers to the finishing and smoothing of the ware with tools after the clay has dried to a leather-hard stage. Since the clay must harden before it can be turned, it is not possible to finish a piece in one sitting.

It is extremely difficult to describe these operations. This is probably the reason why so little has been written about the techniques of throwing and turning. And no matter how much instruction you read, you will not master the use of the wheel except by watching an experienced potter at work and then practicing on your own wheel for

Craftool kick (treadle) wheel sells for about $130, has large working pan, is easy to operate.

75

Harold Castor, head of th
Sculptors and Ceramic Wor
shop, New York City, den
onstrates here how a wid
necked bowl is thrown on
wheel. Widely known as on
of this country's leadin
ceramists, he often appea
on leading network TV show
and his students come fro
all over the world to lea
Workshop's famed method

many hours. There are, for example, a thousand and one little tricks in the position of the arms, hands, thumbs and fingers which are impossible to describe but which can easily be learned by watching an expert throw and turn.

There are dozens of different types of potter's wheels, ranging from the simple kick wheel to the modern electrically driven ones which are rather expensive but are adaptable to many uses because of the numerous accessories that come with them. The kick wheel is suitable for beginners. It can be purchased inexpensively or is easily constructed in any home workshop. The wheel head is set atop a steel shaft. A horizontal-moving treadle is attached to the bottom of the shaft. A simple wood or steel framework holds the shaft in an upright position. By moving the treadle with your foot, the wheel head is made to spin. You can slow down or speed up the wheel by varying your kicking.

Whatever type of wheel is used it should have a head which can be removed. Several heads can then be provided, one for regular work, one for finishing, and so forth. The head or plate on which the potter works is made of plaster of Paris. You can use plaster bats as wheel heads with lugs or inserts to hold them in place. Unless they are perfectly smooth and level, however, your work may be thrown off. When you have finished a piece, remove the bat and leave the soft ware on it to dry. Then you'll be able to throw more models on fresh bats as the first is drying.

Throwing

The first rule of successful throwing is to make sure your clay is properly wedged. This is of utmost importance. The clay must have an even texture and be absolutely free of air bubbles and foreign matter. The smallest bubble can be enough to throw your work off. Once a piece loses its shape in throwing, discard it for a new piece of good clay and start again.

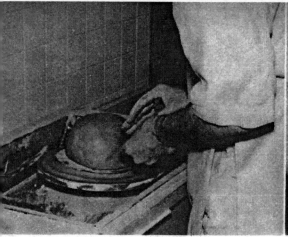

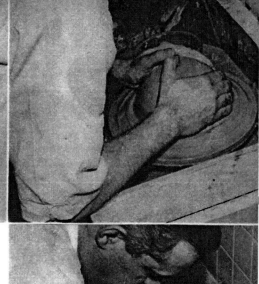

Throw the clay down firmly so that it adheres to center of the wheel. Wheel goes counterclockwise from 200 to 300 rpm. Keep hands and clay moist; water acts as lubricant between hands and clay.

Top right, first hand position is with hands cupped, bringing clay toward center of wheel slowly and firmly. Moisten clay continuously. Arms of the potter should be firmly established on rim of splash pan so that irregularities in piece on wheel can be evened out. Practice this procedure.

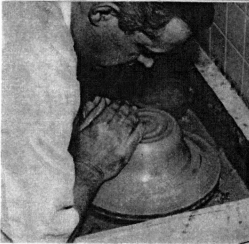

Second hand position, at right, is with the right hand held so that the palm is vertical, and with the left hand horizontal, parallel to top. With gentle pressure, form the cylinder top and sides.

Before you begin throwing, you must check to see if the bat is both clean enough and moist enough to be used. Plunge it in water and soak it nearly to saturation. If the bat surface remains wet one minute after removing it from the water it has soaked too long and must be dried a little. On a too wet bat, the clay slips and cannot be held in one place. If the bat is too dry, the clay will stick and cannot be moved when required. The proper dampness is secured when the clay can be pushed along the surface of the bat without slipping too easily. Experiment and experience will tell you when the bat is properly moist.

Place a basin of water close at hand. As you throw the clay, you will have to keep it wet by splashing water on it. This will make the clay softer and easier to work while it spins. Again, experience alone can tell you how much water to use on the ware you are throwing. Too much moisture will cause the piece to collapse; too little makes shaping almost impossible.

Take a ball of well-wedged clay about three inches in diameter. In placing clay on the bat, slap it down fairly hard, as near to the center of the wheel as you can judge. Start the wheel spinning at a rapid speed. As the wheel is revolving, put both hands on the clay. You are now ready for the first step in throwing, called centering.

As the clay turns under your hands, you will feel its unevenness. The object of centering is to eliminate this vibration, so that as the wheel and clay revolve there is no thumping against your fingers. Your hands on the clay will cause the rotation to slow down rapidly. But before the wheel stops spinning, remove your hands and splash water on the clay as a lubricant. Keep the wheel spinning at as constant a speed as possible, adding water whenever you feel too much friction between the clay and your hands. Press the ball of clay firmly with both hands until you get the feel of the clay running smoothly.

Brace the left elbow against your side

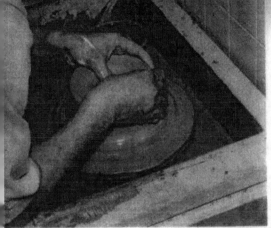

After the cylinder has been formed, place one hand on each side of the clay, with thumbs in center. Exerting a gentle downward pressure, force the thumbs downward. See photo below.

Right, left hand is kept parallel to the left side. Cross the right hand and then project fingers into the hollow formed by the thumbs. Interior is widened and brought out to its desired diameter by holding left hand firm. As can be seen in photo, cylinder begins to grow.

and, wetting the hand, press the ball of the thumb and the lower part of the palm against the clay. Keep the left forearm rigid. Use the right hand to sprinkle water on the clay. You will notice that the clay is thus forced into the center of the wheel.

With the fingers of the right hand pull the clay toward you, at the same time pressing inward with the left hand. As the hands come together the clay will rise into a cone. Do not pull it upward but let it rise of its own accord as it is squeezed. Now bring the hands over the top and, with the thumbs together, press down again. Lumps and irregularities will be felt in the clay and the operations of spinning up and down must be continued until these disappear. All the time you are working with the clay, keep it liberally sprinkled with water.

Let's assume that you are throwing a vase. This calls for a cylindrical shape. Your clay must be properly centered, however, before you can model anything on the wheel. Always start your wheel turning before you start working with your

hands and always remove your hands while the wheel is still running. If you remove your hands after the wheel has stopped you are likely to throw the piece out of line.

Now moisten both hands and clay. Grasp the clay lightly but with sufficient force to give you dominance over the clay. You will find it helpful to steady your hands some way. Brace your elbows against your hips, or use arm supports if necessary. Do not bend your wrists.

Encircle the clay with your hands. Press the right thumb firmly toward the palm to form a cup-shaped hollow. Raise the right hand slowly, still keeping a light pressure on the clay with the thumb. The clay will rise with your hand. Now insert the two first fingers of the left hand into the hollow and hold them against the wall. Slacken the speed of the wheel a bit. Bend the forefinger of the right hand and press the second joint and the knuckle against the outer wall to oppose the fingers which are inside. Press the thumbs together to

In photo at left the left hand is shown palm opened, and two outside fingers (second and index) of right hand are supporting the clay piece. Position then changes to one below.

After photo step above, left-hand index finger is wrapped around the thumb, and right hand applies gentle pressure. Now lift clay cylinder evenly and surely. This process is repeated until desired height is reached. At each pass of the wheel, the cylinder rises.

steady the hands and raise both hands upward together. The fingers inside and outside the clay should be kept at a definite distance apart so that as the hands rise, the clay wall is brought to a uniform thickness. The thumbs must go straight down or the walls will flare out. Be sure to leave enough clay at the bottom to make a base.

Repeat the action of the fingers inside and out. Begin at the bottom and take a closer grip of the clay and draw up the walls as before. At all times have your fingers directly opposite each other with a wall of clay between them, and your right thumb resting lightly on the top rim. Give the clay a chance to adjust itself as you move your fingers. The thinner you make the wall, the taller will be the cylinder. If you feel any place in the wall that is slightly thicker or thinner, exert more pressure for a thick place and less for a thin place.

Once you have started the movement from bottom to top, carry it through to completion. You can feel the roll of clay moving to the top. If you stop before reaching the top, you will leave a ridge of thickness where you stop. Even if you strive to keep the walls of the cylinder exactly the same thickness from top to bottom, the base and lower part of the wall will be slightly thicker. This is how it should be, since this part will be cut away on the outside in the turning or trimming process.

Never lose control of the top edge of the cylinder. The weight of your right thumb gently resting on the top edge is enough to keep it even. At no time exert too great a pressure any place except in the first centering. Let the wheel do most of the work. If you prefer a curved or tapered wall on the vase instead of a straight vertical wall, apply slight pressure where needed. If you want the top of the wall to flare outward, for example, hold the fingers of your left hand against the inside surface, keeping the right hand directly opposite on the outside for support. For a concave curve, press the outside surface of the wall with the right

In top photo at left, Harold Castor begins the shaping of the cylinder and the bowl now shows signs of taking its eventual, and graceful, form.

Above, rim is formed by holding second and third fingers of left hand on inside of bowl, at top. Thumb and first finger of right hand are outside and just below rim of bowl. By applying a little pressure on the fingers inside bowl, form clay over right-hand thumb and finger, to make the lip.

By resting the right-hand wrist on the splash pan you can keep fingers in bow-like position; left hand holds right one to steady it. Now form hip.

Castor desired to give hip portion of vase a texture. Decoration can be added later on and can be highly effective over areas previously treated in this manner. To achieve a texture, apply a saw-toothed blade tool, or even a piece of hacksaw blade, to outside of piece while it is revolving.

When the piece has dried to a leather-hard condition, you are ready to cut the foot. The ware is centered on the potter's wheel upside down, and is anchored securely in place with several pieces of moist clay. Foot is formed by cutting off excess clay, leaving rim of desired diameter.

hand, keeping the left inside for support. To widen the top, so that the wall is straight but not vertical, hold your hand lightly against the entire length of the inside surface, at the same time supporting the outside. This is a delicate procedure and is not recommended for the beginner.

It is not possible to finish work to perfection by throwing. The clay is too soft to handle and for proper finishing the piece must be turned over to get at the bottom. For this the clay must be leather-hard. As soon as the piece is thrown, wipe off the excess moisture, remove the bat from the wheel head and allow the ware to stand until it can support itself. As the piece begins to dry, it will separate from the bat. Now place the leather-hard vase upon a clean bat. You are now ready to turn the vase.

Turning

If you have left sufficient clay at the base, you can turn a small foot—that is, hollow out the bottom slightly, leaving a rim around the outside for the vase to rest on. First look inside the vase and study the curve in the bottom. This is the general contour you should try to cut on the outside of the base. Pick up the vase and lightly mark on the bottom the width of the foot to be cut. Try to remember the curve of the inside bottom so that you may cut enough from the outside to conform to the inside curve.

Turn the vase upside down on the new bat. Your first problem is to center the piece on the wheel. A pencil line may be drawn on the bat. Hold the pencil at the edge of the vase where it touches the bat and rotate the wheel slowly, holding the pencil in this position to make a circle slightly larger than the vase. Check to see if the piece is perfectly centered by doing this: Take the pencil in your hand and steady your arm by holding it firmly against your side. Let the point of the pencil barely touch the vase. Turn the vase slowly. If the vase is centered properly the pencil will touch it at all places as it rotates. If the piece is off-center, carefully move it until the pencil does touch at all points. Hold the vase in place by pressing at least three clay balls around the perimeter. These will keep the vase in place when the wheel is rotated. Otherwise centrifugal force would send it flying off the bat.

Start the wheel spinning rapidly. With a cutting tool, starting at the center of the base and working out, cut out to the mark you made for the foot. Don't cut too deeply at first. It is better to go back and cut again. Use the tip of your tool and cut at right angles to the bottom of the vase. If the wheel is not turning fast enough you will be plagued with ridges. Keep your wrist firm and hold the tool steady.

A small rim about one-quarter of an inch thick should be left for the vase to stand

Cross-sectional view of turned vase shows how thickness of walls are controlled by finger pressure.

From "Craftsmanship in Clay" by Karl Martz

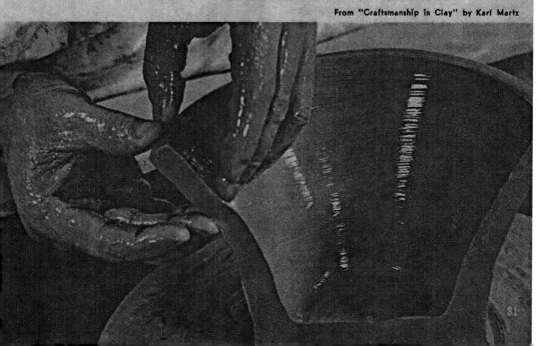

on. Trim a contour on the lower outside which follows the inside curve.

An experienced thrower reduces the final work to a minimum. The more expert you become at throwing a piece the less cutting you will have to do when turning, except at the base. Do not expect to correct or remove throwing defects when you are turning. A piece must be thrown correctly if you want a worth-while ware upon its completion.

After you are satisfied with the foot you have cut, clean the vase with a damp sponge while it is still spinning on the wheel. Apply the sponge to inside and outside surfaces to smooth off small pieces of clay and to dampen the wall slightly, which makes it easier to see how much additional cutting is necessary. Use a thin, flat, wet sponge, which you rest upon your fingers and work over the surface of the vase just as though the sponge weren't there. Never dab with the sponge. If more cutting is necessary, use the sponge again to remove the tool marks. Be sure you do not gouge or score too deeply.

If the piece requires a spout or a handle, these can be formed by the coil method and welded in place with mending slip. You may, if you wish, leave the marks that denote wheel work, or these may be fettled off with a damp sponge while rotating the wheel.

Do not expect to become an expert with the potter's wheel overnight. It requires much practice. There is, however, no reason why you shouldn't develop enough facility with the wheel to produce excellent wares after a while. All it takes is patience and determination. And the result, you'll find, is more than worth the effort. For there is nothing quite like the thrill you'll feel while transforming a lump of clay beneath your hands into a beautiful ceramic ware.

These directions cover the general principles, but everyone will find ways of holding his hands or working the clay that will be more comfortable for him. No two potters use the wheel in precisely the same way. But all of them stick closely to these basic rules for working with the wheel. Two or three hours of watching a ceramist throwing and turning will teach you more than a dozen books on the subject. If at all possible, visit a studio which is equipped with a wheel and see how it is used. At least be certain to study the step-by-step photos on these pages before you actually start throwing. •

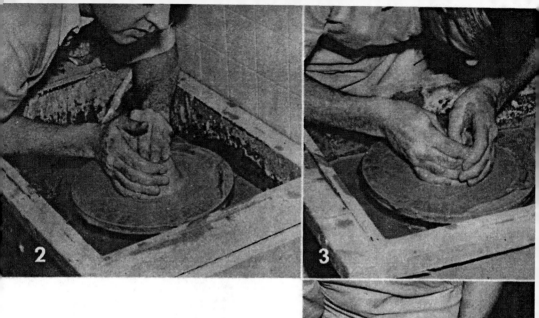

how to throw a
SMALL BOWL

In the preceding series of photos you noted how the positioning of hands in throwing will shape a clay piece. Here, Castor shows you the basic steps of throwing by demonstrating a small bowl.

Step 1. Adhere the clay firmly
Step 2. Center the clay
Step 3. Make the hole
Step 4. Open the hole
Step 5. Start the cylinder
Step 6. Lift the cylinder
Step 7. Form the small bowl
Step 8. Finish the lip

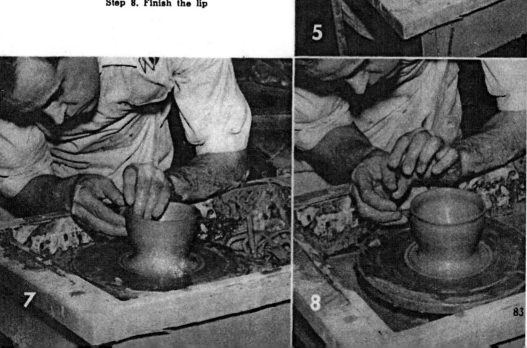

decorating your ware

Effective decoration is the essence of fine ceramics craftsmanship. Practice this variety of techniques.

THERE ARE many effective techniques by which you can decorate the wares you produce in your ceramic workshop. Decorations may be applied upon soft clay by incising, inlaying and embossing; upon dry clay and bisque-fired clay by color, either under the glaze or with no glaze at all; in the glaze by the use of colors or colored glazes; or over the glaze with colors and enamels and decalcomanias. Each of these methods has its own special features. Each has its own possibilities and limitations which should be mastered.

The simplest, but not necessarily the least effective, form of decoration consists of scratching a design in the model while it is still soft. All that is required in the way of tools is a scratch-point, a darning needle, a toothpick, or any other pointed object which can be used as a stylus. The clay should be leather-hard when you incise your design. You can make just a line drawing, either naturalistic or abstract, or you can bring the design out in relief by cutting away part of the background.

The next logical step is sgraffito decora-

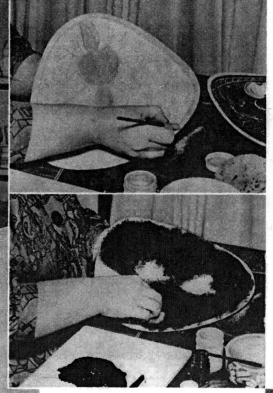

Far left, decorated greenware plate has been fired in kiln at 1850° F (cone 06). Upon removal, finished plate is ready to use. First step in decorating plate is to mask larger areas of design which are to receive no color during process. Masking compound, applied to cleaned greenware following rough pencil sketch, is water-soluble and normally applied by brush; it may be used on artware, porcelain greenware or bisque, and after glazes are applied the compound peels off. Here, the border and center fruit areas are masked.

With water-based color, sponge is used to dab desired color on the entire piece of greenware. Color won't penetrate masked-off areas, and is kept at even consistency by adding water until it's easily put on with sponge without running or clotting. Greenware is more fragile than fired ceramics, so support it from underneath with hand rather than holding it at the edges.

To obtain fine white lines seen on the finished piece a sharp-pointed sgraffito tool is used, as at right. Exert firm pressure on tool to scratch through thin coat of color to greenware itself. This technique is easy, and any mistakes can be simply corrected by sponging over the scratched areas with the original color any number of times.

tion. To do this, cover the whole piece with a coating of contrasting colored slip. Then carefully scratch a design through the outer slip, exposing the clay underneath.

Use a large brush to paint the slip on the leather-hard unfired clay. Some ceramists prefer to dip the piece into a large container of slip, but this is generally not practical for the hobbyist because of the large quantity of slip required. It may be advisable first to lightly sketch the design to be etched in pencil. When you are done carving the sgraffito design, let the piece dry

Above, after color is sponged on and design scratched in, masking compound is removed simply by pricking the surface with sharp point of tool and then peeling off the masking. Don't leave masking on for longer than six hours.

Final decorating stage is shading of fruits, and internal shading effects. This is achieved by using same color as in background, toned down with water. Just brush on, and to change a brush stroke employ water-dampened sponge.

Satisfaction and accomplishment are your rewards when you open the top of the kiln to inspect your finished and successful pieces. Kiln shown is low-cost and small; larger models which hold sizable pieces cost around $45.

thoroughly. Bisque-fire it before applying a transparent glaze, and then fire it again.

A similar sgraffito method is this: Incise your design *before* adding a coat of colored slip. Then paint the slip *over* the design. Finally, scrape the slip off the surface, leaving only that which has settled in the incisions you scratched, so that the lines of the design are contrasted with the clay body. Wonderful effects can be accomplished with experimentation. For example, all the outer slip need not be removed, but instead left here and there on the piece as colorful highlights. Usually, the slip is not painted over the entire surface but only over the area which has been incised.

The use of colored slip need not be restricted to sgraffito work. On the contrary, slip painting—otherwise known as *engobe* decoration—is employed to obtain many types of wonderful designs.

Any light colored slip, or engobe, can be tinted by the addition of metal oxides, stains or underglaze colors (these are explained later in this chapter), then used to paint designs on leather-hard or dry objects. One color may be placed over another color and shaded or blended into harmonizing designs. This can often be combined beautifully with sgraffito work.

You can also use engobes for slip-trailing. Fill a small rubber syringe with engobe and squeeze the slip through the nozzle in a thin line while tracing a design on the surface to be decorated, as a pastry chef squeezes out cake designs. By means of slip-trailing, you can shape delicate flowers and leaves of clay, just as they are formed of cake icing in a bake shop. For a gorgeous mosaic effect, an irregular crisscross, or checkerboard, patterns can be drawn and filled in with contrasting colors, then glazed with a transparent glaze.

If you have admired the elegant wares made by Wedgwood, here is an easy way to attain similarly good-looking results. Take a mold which has a cameo or floral design and brush slip on this portion of the mold. Now take a different color slip and pour it into the mold as usual. When you remove the castware from the mold, the two colors of slip will have hardened into one piece, but the main body of the piece will be one color and the relief design another.

It is also possible and worth while to pour a decorative mold in one color slip and the main body of a model in another color. This is the way in which genuine Wedgwood is manufactured. The white figures which stand out in relief against the famous blue background are separately cast. Then, when leather-hard they are slip-glued in place on the piece to be decorated. Such separately cast ornaments are called *sprigging*. With a little practice, you should be able to apply sprigging to your own castware without difficulty.

Most colored slip can be purchased from ceramics suppliers, although it is not too complicated a matter to mix your own colors. Many engobes are naturally colored clay. The temperature to which an engobe is exposed will often affect its color tremendously. Victorian clay, for example, turns to a rich mahogany at medium-high temperatures, while at low temperatures it becomes a lustrous black. Dalton No. 93 becomes brick red in the kiln, turning darker as the temperature mounts. If you learn the effects of heat on the engobes you use, you will be able to control their color and obtain any shade you desire. The best way to learn is to experiment, keeping records of your results. Next best, perhaps faster but certainly less interesting, is to study a technical treatise on the chemistry of ceramics. Of course, an instructor or supplier will be happy to answer specific questions about any clay.

To make your own engobe colors, you will have to add small quantities of metallic oxides to the slip. Keep in mind that one-third of slip by weight is water. The percentages given here for the amount of oxide needed to produce the desired color are based on the dry ingredients of the slip by weight. In other words, if you had 100 grams of slip and wanted to tint it blue, 66⅔ grams are comprised of dry ingredients. Add three percent cobalt oxide (see chart), or two grams, since three percent of 66⅔ equals two.

Divide the total weight of slip, excluding the vessel in which it is weighed, and divide by two-thirds *before* figuring the amount of oxide you will need. Mix the oxide and the slip thoroughly and strain several times through a 160-mesh screen.

The combinations and different types of coloring agents are virtually unlimited, but on the next page is a basic list of oxides, percentages which should be used, and the colors they will produce.

This list, complete as far as it goes, is designed only to illustrate how colored engobes are made. Many oxides are capable of imparting more than one color, depending upon how much of each is used, in what combination with other oxides, and at what temperature they are fired. Iron oxide, for instance, can be utilized to obtain green and red engobes, as well as brown and black. Copper can be used for red, green

Interesting sponging method uses rotating electric table to spin greenware as color steadily is "wiped" from inside to outside of plate, to leave the spiralling lines heavier in the center.

Here is reverse effect, with heavier area around outside. Plate is lifted from the table and an additional design in a darker color is superimposed by brush on previously applied underglaze.

and blue engobes. Chromium oxide imparts a hue of green, pink or red. Silver oxide is used in gray and yellow engobes. Until the advent of the atomic bomb, uranium found its biggest commercial use in tinting engobes yellow, green and ivory. Today understandably enough, it is not available to ceramists. But the same colors can be produced with other oxides.

Metallic Oxide	Percent by Weight (of dry ingredients)	Color
Cobalt oxide	3%	Blue
Cobalt oxide	3%	
and Nickel oxide	1%	Blue
Cobalt oxide	2%	
and Iron oxide	1%	Warm blue
Copper oxide	8%	Green
Copper oxide	5%	
and Cobalt oxide	1%	Blue green
Antimony oxide	8%	Yellow
Iron oxide	7%	Brown
Manganese oxide	6%	Brown
Manganese iron oxide	10%	Black

There are several other substances besides metallic oxides which can be used to color slips and engobes. A dried and powdered clay such as Albany can be mixed with a lighter slip to turn it a reddish brown. Cadmium sulfide will make an engobe turn yellow, as will lead antimonate. Orange can be produced by mixing in lead

chromate. Sulfur is useful for obtaining an amber hue. Various gold compounds will impart colors of red, rose, purple and gold.

Engobes should be brushed on the surface evenly and to the approximate thickness of one-sixteenth inch if a solid color is desired, otherwise there will be the possibility of uneven color after the glaze-firing. If a glaze is put over this slip, it will probably produce an uneven color after it is fired if the slip is uneven in thickness. If slip is applied too thickly, however, it will tend to crack and break away from the surface of the object. Whenever you use one clay over another you should be certain the fire shrinkage is the same. Generally a dark-colored engobe or slip is applied to a lighter clay body, although the reverse can be done with topnotch results. When a light engobe is brushed over a dark clay, the latter is partially seen through the coating in the thinnest places. Many ceramists thus obtain fine shadow effects in their slip-painted designs.

Engobe coloring is frequently used to color the inside of a ware with one shade and the outside with another. Variations can also be made by adding a colored design and leaving a band of natural clay to show them. Then, with one application of transparent glaze, either gloss or matte, you will give the appearance of an interestingly constructed and decorated piece. By glaz-

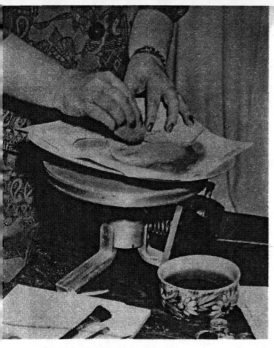

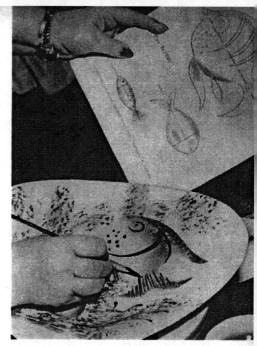

Simple but very effective decorating technique is that of stencil. First, piece of greenware is covered with paper stencil, then colors prepared on board are dabbed into open areas with sponge.

Stencil removed, design is completed by brushing color on to accent the appearance. From start to finish of this design took only 1½ minutes—and the final product is both pleasing, unusual.

ing only a slip-painted design and leaving the rest of the piece to fire as bisque, you can produce a ware which seems to be inset with jewels.

It is extremely difficult to separate the glazing process from that of decorating, since these two steps so often overlap. The most commonly used forms of decoration are underglazing and overglazing. Underglaze decoration includes any ornamentation that is applied to ware before it is glazed and fired. This includes slip-painting and sgraffito carving or any color painting done on greenware or bisque. For example, if you were to paint a floral design on a piece of greenware, then cover your work with a clear glaze and fire, it would be a typical form of underglazed decoration.

Such ornamentation applied after the ware is glazed is called overglaze decoration. The two most popular forms of overglaze decoration are hand-painting with overglaze colors and the use of decalcomanias, or decals.

The main difference between underglaze and overglaze colors is that the former are not fusible. That is, they will not adhere to the ware even if fired. They will still be a powder and will rub off. Glaze is necessary to hold the colors in place and keep them from smearing. Underglaze colors consist of one-third metallic oxide, one-

third slip and one-third glaze. Make certain that the slip in the paint is the same clay as that in the piece to be decorated so it will have the same shrinkage in the kiln. The glaze in the color must also be the same glaze that will be used over the underglaze paint. Some ceramists prefer to add the glaze after the color has been applied to the greenware. Either method is satisfactory. If you do not want to mix glaze in the original color formula, you can spray a thin coating over the decoration with an atomizer.

Underglaze colors can be made in the home workshop, but it is much more prudent and timesaving for the novice to buy them already prepared. Virtually any desired color can be bought at a reasonable price. By mixing the commercially prepared colors yourself, your paint palette can include every color on the spectrum. Always read the directions which come with the paints—and then experiment to your heart's content.

When using underglaze colors on bisque ware, rather than greenware, no slip or glaze should be added to the color mixture. This is because the bisque has been completely preshrunk in the drying and firing processes and the slip in the colors has not. Unequal shrinkage would thus result, causing the paint to crack and peel off.

Use ordinary water-color brushes to ap-

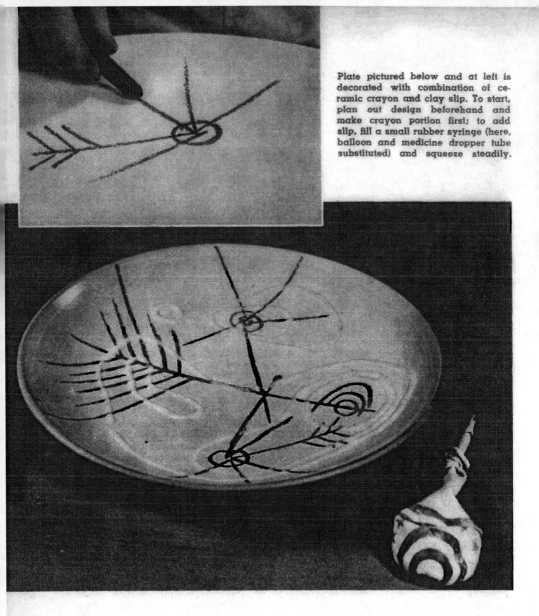

Plate pictured below and at left is decorated with combination of ceramic crayon and clay slip. To start, plan out design beforehand and make crayon portion first; to add slip, fill a small rubber syringe (here, balloon and medicine dropper tube substituted) and squeeze steadily.

ply underglaze colors. A good selection of brushes would range in size from No. 00 up to Nos. 11 or 12. Both pointed-tip brushes and flat brushes will prove useful. The greenware should be completely dry before it is decorated with underglaze colors, otherwise there is no absorption and the color will be too thin on the surface. Keep the brush well loaded with paint and let the color flow on the piece. Never drag the brush across the clay, since brush strokes will show through the glaze after it is fired. It is better to paint over solid-color areas three or four times to make sure the color has been applied heavy enough. It is all right to paint thin color over color.

Underglaze decorations can also be applied to greenware with a spray gun. Many commercial potteries use this method. Cut a design in a paper stencil and place it against the surface to be decorated. Using a thin spray, aim the gun at the openings in the stencil. Any number of colors may be used and many different shading effects can be accomplished. For most hobbyists, however, the cost of spray-gun decorating is prohibitive. You will need such equipment as a spraying booth, turntable, spray gun and compressor.

For line designs on flat pieces, such as tiles and trays, you can effectively apply underglaze paints with a small rubber

After basic design is coated with melted paraffin or wax, contrasting colored slip is brushed over entire surface of ware; this is called "wax-resist" method since clay slip will not adhere to the painted surfaces and wax will fire-out in kiln. Slip mixed with powdered engobes will vary colors.

Photos from "Craftsmanship in Clay"

With any scratching or sgraffito tool, incise your design to depth of 1/32 to 1/64 inch; don't make all lines of same width and never go over a line.

Using thin rolls of clay, drape them on ware in approximate or permanent position; design can be worked into the clay rope with a modeling tool.

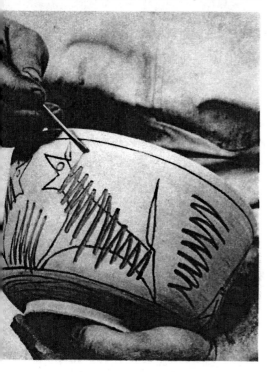

In commercial production, raised gold is used for decoration generally on only very elaborate patterns. Skillful craftsman applies it by hand after all other decoration is completed. It is given very low fire to fuse the gold onto the ware; too high a kiln firing would destroy the gold.

Below, embossed or hand-applied clay bas-reliefs made from a press mold by the "figure maker" are being applied to ware by the ornamenter. Surface of clay ware is moistened with water and ornament is fixed by skillful pressure of finger. A sensitive touch is necessary to avoid accidental marring of fine ornament detail.

Wedgwood photos

syringe. On round pieces it is much more difficult to control the flow of color. Several different colors can be kept at hand in different syringes. For best results, apply the paint freely in swirls and straight lines. If you wish, of course, you can work out your design beforehand, although this is apt to make the finished pattern look too stiff and mechanical.

It is possible to achieve lovely decorative effects by combining underglaze colors with colored glazes. But a clear glaze is usually selected if underglaze paint has been used.

There is a distinct difference between underglaze and overglaze colors. Overglaze paints, for the most part, are oil-based paints. They are applied after the piece has been glazed and fired. After the decoration is placed on the glaze, the piece has to be fired again at a low temperature to make the decorations permanent.

Overglaze paints can be obtained from any ceramics supply house. They can be easily combined to form new, secondary colors on a glass or porcelain slab. Add a few drops of turpentine to the paint and mix before using, with a palette knife, until it is smooth. Too much turpentine will make the paint too thin. Some potters argue that fat oil is a better paint thinner than turpentine. A better grade brush is required for overglaze colors, since they must be cleaned in turpentine after they are used. This will cause a cheap brush to stiffen and fall apart after it has been used a few times. A sable-tipped brush is recommended. Do not worry if loose bristles are pulled from the brush and remain in the paint while you apply the color. The hairs will burn away in the kiln and no trace of them will remain.

Photos by author

It is important to measure out by weight all of your dry powders, and see that they are combined and mixed in a mortar and pestle very thoroughly.

When completing decoration on any large surface, always fill in what looks to be "bare" area with varied lines, scratching through engobe coating.

When you are finished painting the design on the glaze, let the paint dry before firing. To develop deep, rich, jewel-like colors, you will have to paint on one coat, fire it, and then paint on another coat of the same color and fire again. This can be done many times until you have achieved the color you are looking for. Liquid gold and silver can be painted over other colors after they have been fired: apply the gold or silver and fire again.

Overglaze colors and gold and silver have very low firing temperatures. Some will burn off at 1000 degrees Fahrenheit. Most, however, require a temperature of approximately 1300 degrees to mature properly. If the kiln does get too hot, no permanent damage is usually done. Most of the overglaze colors will merely burn off and disappear. You can then redecorate the piece and fire properly. Many ceramists over-fire a piece on purpose when they wish to change or correct a design.

Decalcomanias, or decals, are used extensively as overglaze decorations by commercial potteries. The designs are printed in color specifically prepared for use in ceramic ware by transfer. Decals can be purchased from supply firms, and most come complete with directions. First coat the glazed ware with a sizing of balsam and turpentine. Allow the sizing to dry until it is tacky. Place the decal against the tacky surface to which it will adhere. Dampen, then remove the paper, leaving the design on the ware. Firing will make the decoration quite permanent.

Decals can also be applied to bisque, or unglazed, ware. Dilute regular decal varnish with 40% to 50% turpentine and spread a thin coat on the surface of the bisque ware that is to be decorated. When the varnish has become tacky, lay the decal in place, face down. If the decal has been printed on duplex paper, you must first remove the tissue from the heavy backing paper. Once the decal is in the proper position, rub with a stiff brush which has been moistened. Remove all creases and bubbles. Apply water until the tissue paper floats away. Never *pull* the paper.

Fast overtaking these varnish-mounted decals in popularity among hobbyists are watermount decals, a more recent innovation which are printed with a ceramic overglaze and merely requires the use of water for transferring. Until these watermount decals were introduced, few home-studio ceramists used decals for decorating their wares. The method of application is comparatively simple. Any glazed surface is satisfactory. Before applying the decal, make sure the ware is free of all fingerprints and other greasy marks.

Cut the individual decal out and immerse in water for about 20 seconds, or until the clear film is free to slide from the backing paper. The design is then placed in position on the ware, face up, and the backing paper is slipped out from under the color film. Smooth down with sponge or your fingers, pressing from the center toward the edges. In this way remove all excess water from underneath the surface of the decal. Decals must adhere perfectly to glazed surfaces or tiny holes will burn in the pattern. Dry thoroughly before firing, at least 24 hours. •

using an airbrush

The following material is reprinted from the book "Airbrush in Ceramics" (Copyright 1955 by Graphicraft Publications) by gracious consent of the author, J. Zellers Allen. Mr. Allen directs The Allen Airbrush Institute in Detroit and has won nation-wide recognition for his work in ceramic techniques.

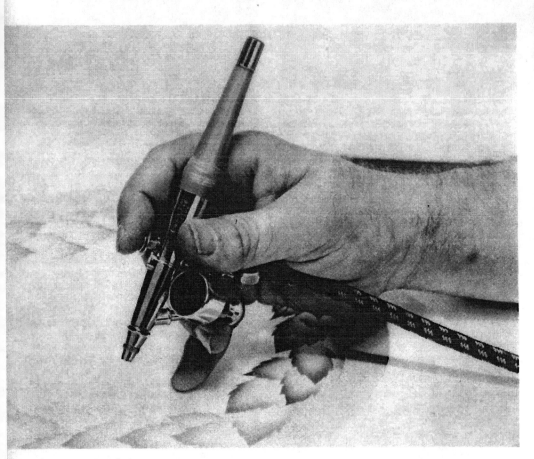

AN airbrush, quite simply, is a small paint or color spray gun. There are two general types of airbrushes: single-action and double-action.

A double-action airbrush derives its name from the fact that the control lever has two actions: down for the release of air, and back for release of color. As will be easily understood, this double action enables the operator to increase or decrease the flow of color during a stroke, which is a distinct advantage, and which is the feature that enables an artist to really create with airbrush. In using a double action airbrush the lever is pushed all the way down in releasing air, because it is not the type of valve that permits any regulation other than open or closed. The control is not always pulled all the way back in releasing the color, because the amount of color released depends on the extent to which this lever is pulled back. For a little color, pull back a little; for more color, pull back more.

A single-action airbrush gets its name from the fact that the small finger lever, used to control the flow of air and color, has only one action, up and down—or, more accurately, down and up. You push the lever down and, when you release it, a spring pushes it back up. When depressed, this control releases both air and color. The control for the amount of the color released is located elsewhere on the brush and must be adjusted to the operator's liking or requirements previous to activating the control lever. This is a disadvantage despite the fact that some advertising carries the statement: "Air and color controls are independent of each other," as though it were advantageous.

From the foregoing brief descriptions, it is obvious that the double-action airbrush is the more versatile of the two. This factor should be kept in mind when choosing an airbrush for ceramic use as well as for any other purpose.

If you buy a single-action brush, there will come a time when its lack of versatility and flexibility will hold you back, and you will be sorry that you did not get a double-action brush. If you choose a double-action brush it will last you a lifetime, with proper care, and its only limitation will be your imagination and your continually growing ability to handle it. You will find that the difference in price is not great, and that the difference in what you will be able to accomplish with it is entirely out of proportion to the slight additional cost.

Frankly, there is not much to learn about the operation of a single-action brush that is not covered by the instruction leaflet that came with it. What more there is to learn about it will be covered by the instructions presented in this book, except that the owner of a single-action brush will have to substitute the separate adjustment of his brush for the pull-back of the double-action brush.

Two general types of air supply are available for airbrush use: *compressed air* and *carbonic gas*. Of these, the air compressor is the more popular and practical.

It is a very sound idea to buy the best air compressor you can afford. Your airbrush work will be no better than your air supply will allow it to be. You probably won't need the largest compressor you can find, but you will never regret buying a good one—one that will adequately handle the brush, or brushes, you may wish to use.

The other practical air supply, liquid carbonic gas, is more expensive than a compressor, in the long run, but has the advantage of being silent and clean. Carbon dioxide in twenty-pound cylinders may be obtained in any locality having soda fountains—and what localities do not have them? A pressure gauge and regulator, to permit the use of gas for airbrush purposes, may be purchased from your local ceramic or art supply store. Full directions for attaching it to a standard cylinder of CO_2 will accompany the regulator if it is one that was supplied by one of the airbrush companies. Read them carefully and follow them to the letter.

Regardless of the kind of air supply used, cleanliness and care in its use are as desirable as in the use of your airbrush.

One point, which seems to be very pertinent in the application of airbrush to any kind of work, needs to be made right here: Airbrush finds its greatest use in conjunction with other methods of color application! So, you see, you are not to throw away your red sable brushes and your sgraffito tools, because you will be using them right along with the airbrush—if you use the airbrush properly.

Airbrush does, very easily, many of the things that are extremely difficult to do with other methods. On the other hand, certain things can be done much better with your regular methods than with airbrush! A blend, which one can achieve almost without effort with the airbrush, is not easy with regular brushes; whereas, a sharp definite line of solid color is usually difficult with the airbrush, but easy with regular brushes. Airbrush will supplement your other tools, not replace them.

Obviously, if you were learning to be a dressmaker, you would not do your practicing on expensive silk or satin. Neither does it appear sensible to practice airbrush on greenware or bisque. Confine your first airbrush work to the cheapest of paper, secure in the knowledge that when you have mastered it sufficiently to apply it to a pot, the clay surface, raw or bisqued, will ac-

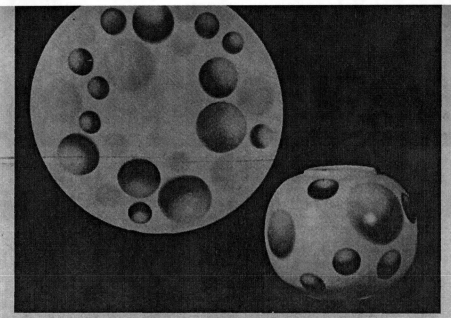

cept the color just as well, and sometimes better, than the paper surface.

There is an old Allenism in airbrush instruction to the effect that the one absolutely essential thing in the making of a good airbrush user is a large wastebasket! Don't spare the paper.

How to Hold and Operate Airbrush

If you hold a pencil in the most common way, that is, resting on your middle finger between the first joint and the end of the finger, held there by a downward pressure of the tip of the forefinger, a downward and to the right pressure of the thumb, you need only substitute the airbrush for the pencil to have the proper hold on it; the only difference is that instead of pressing downward on the body of the airbrush, as with a pencil, you place the tip of the forefinger against the small control lever projecting from the top of the airbrush barrel.

Examine the accompanying photographs carefully. You will find that this grip will allow very easy manipulation of the control lever. A downward pressure of the lever, the first necessary action of this control in every instance, is very naturally accomplished. The "pull back" to release color, while not so natural to a pencil user, is, nevertheless, not out of keeping with the position and the grip.

Refer frequently to the photograph showing the proper way to hold the airbrush. Notice the position of the individual fingers, especially the forefinger. Greater control is possible if the forefinger is kept slightly bowed, or tense, at all times, even when the control lever is completely forward and not releasing color.

It is literally true that you work in three dimensions with the airbrush. You must work to and from the surface to which you are applying color as well as back and forth across it. This leads to slightly further complication when working on curved surfaces of pottery, which, of course, is another reason for mastering the technicalities of airbrush on paper.

Synchronization

There are five factors to synchronize when operating an airbrush. They are:

1. The "push down" for air.
2. The "pull back" for color.
3. The distance of the airbrush from the receiving surface.
4. The direction of the stroke being made.
5. The speed with which the airbrush is moved.

Let us consider these five factors in order:

1. The Push Down for Air. As mentioned before, you always push all the way down to release the full pressure of air. This valve on the airbrush is not the kind of valve which permits partial air release. If pressure needs changing, it must be done at the source, through the medium of an air regulator which reduces the pressure that is released from the air tank.

2. The Pull Back for Color. This action differs from the push down in that it is not always a completed action—it is not always pulled all the way back. The extent to which this lever is pulled back controls the amount of color released, and since you do not always want to release a full blast of

SPHERES: Pieces shown at left were done with airbrush and stencil. Stencil for a disc or sphere is one of easiest to make. Simply scratch circle into piece of cellulose acetate with pair of sharp-pointed dividers and "crack" out center by bending acetate back and forth. Sphere effect is produced by shading. This is an easy and versatile decoration for first tries.

"SKYSCRAPERS": Similarity of design to city skyline earned this stencil effect its name. At bottom is stencil used. Slots in stencil are airbrushed separately as stencil is shifted around for more interesting result. More of skyline effect is achieved if airbrushed areas overlap. Try monochromatic color scheme, or, say, greens and browns.

color, you do not always pull all the way back on this lever. Restraint is the rule of thumb for activating this lever. Remember this: *You build color with the airbrush.* Seldom is the full intensity of the color achieved with once-over spraying. Repeated light sprayings, permitting that "build up," are more easily controlled and less likely to result in costly errors. It is easy to add color with the airbrush; difficult, if not impossible, to remove it once it has been applied too heavily. Make haste slowly. Speed, if desired, will come with practice.

3. *The Distance of Airbrush from Surface.* The distance of the airbrush from the surface to which you are applying color will regulate the size line or width of spray that you will get. It also helps to determine how far back you can pull on the color release lever. The farther away from the surface, the more you can pull back on the control lever without getting "wet" spots.

Working "wet" is to be avoided, generally, because the same air that applies the color will then cause it to blow outward from the wet area in little rivulets or fingers of moisture. Sometimes this effect can be turned to account.

This advice about working "wet" does not apply when the airbrush is used for all-over application of color or glaze, because, when coating something in this manner, the airbrush, or ware, is kept constantly in motion; consequently, it does not remain in one spot long enough to blow the color. A wet coating for such purposes will give a better finish to the completed ceramic piece.

4. *Direction of the Stroke.* All airbrush

work is done with "strokes." A stroke might be described as the line or area covered from the time the control lever is pulled back to release color until it is pushed forward to stop the flow of color. *To master the making of lines without knobs or splashes is to master the basic airbrush strokes.* Everything you will ever do with the airbrush will be done with this basic stroke. From this it is easy to understand why it is imperative that you master the controlled line. The "direction" of the stroke will determine the results of your airbrushing, exactly the way that the direction in which a pencil point is moved in contact with paper determines the object that is drawn on the paper.

5. *Speed with which Airbrush Is Moved.* The speed with which you move the airbrush over the surface while releasing color will determine the amount of color applied to the surface by the stroke.

Let us say that you make two lines exactly fifteen inches long, with the airbrush exactly the same distance from the paper in both cases, pulling back exactly the same degree to release color for both of the lines. Now, if it takes one second to make the first line, and two seconds to make the second line, you will have applied exactly twice as much color to the second line as you did to the first. The second line will be heavier and darker. The nature of the airbrush is such that, if you pull back on the control lever to release color and keep the brush aimed at one spot, it will proceed to spray every drop of color in the cup on that spot; consequently, the longer it takes to make any given stroke, the more color will be applied during the stroke. ●

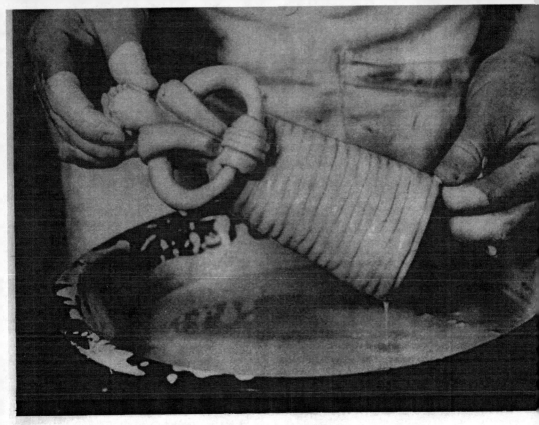

how to use glazes

There's no limit to how much you can know about glazes,
but even the novice can use them with beautiful results.

GLAZES consist of materials which, when subjected to intense heat in a kiln, melt and form a glasslike coating on the surface of the clay. Glazes serve two major functions, utilitarian and decorative. In pottery, the glaze gives a smooth surface, prevents food and water from being absorbed by the clay, and is more easily cleaned. Glazing also gives a more pleasing color and texture than the clay and adds greatly to the beauty of the piece. In sculpture, glazes are not necessary for practical purposes, but sometimes they increase the excitement and interest of such an art object.

The choice of glazes in general, or of a glaze for a particular object, requires considerable knowledge, sensitivity, and experience. For the beginner, commercial glazes which have been carefully checked

for satisfactory results are suggested. If possible, secure your glazes and clays from the same supply source because glazes are designed for specific clays and firing temperatures.

It is vital that you make sure the glaze you use properly fits the body of the clay. Should the clay shrink more in firing than the glaze, for example, whole sections of the glaze will chip off. If the reverse is true, and the glaze shrinks more than the clay, then there will be wide areas on the surface of the piece left unglazed. Do not expect glaze to hide sloppy workmanship. More than likely, it will accent rather than camouflage flaws and blemishes.

Lead oxide and silica in a proportion of 3.7 to 1 will form the simplest kind of glaze. However, it would be very crude and dull yellow in color. Moreover, it would be too

Most widely used methods of glazing large areas are by pouring glaze into item for interior glaze, such as in bottle or jar, and by immersing or dipping entire item into glaze, as with figure at left. Be sure to touch up the spots made by the fingers.

Right, sample ceramic buttons that have been fired with actual glazes to show the finished result are available from most manufacturers of glazes for a few dollars.

If you prefer you can make your own sample glazes rather than buy manufacturer's. Coat a piece of defective greenware with smears of glaze in different colors. Always scratch name of glaze through tile.

To mix your own glazes, purchase a mortar and pestle. Or, for homemade equivalent, use a jar and thick glass swizzle stick. Also handy: a palette knife, glazed tile.

fusible under most heat conditions and would lose its gloss if left in the kiln very long. To counteract these faults, alumina must be added. Fortunately, since pure alumina is hard to obtain, all natural clays contain alumina. Thus, clay, which is plentiful and inexpensive, is added to glazing formulas. From this simple beginning, potters have developed the beautiful and relatively easy-to-use glazes available to hobbyists today.

All glazes contain glasslike or glass ingredients in their basic formulas, which cause the glassy, shiny finish. Color is imparted to a glaze by the addition of metallic oxides. The more clay present in a glaze formula, the duller will be the finish. Glazes can be transparent or opaque, shiny or matte. Transparent glazes are usually applied over all objects which have been slip-decorated, so that the colors and designs may show through. A transparent glaze is not necessarily clear of color. It may be tinted slightly with a small percentage of color agents. Opaque glazes are applied on pieces which have no painted decoration, where it is desirable to have a solid color, or to cover the color of the clay itself. Opaque glazes are sometimes referred to as enamels.

If you wish to change the texture of a shiny glaze to a matte or dull glaze, you can try adding varying amounts of the following materials: bone ash, up to 5%; titanium oxide, up to 5%; zinc oxide, up to 10%; rutile, up to 10%. The materials should be compounded as silicates. The interesting texture of matte glazes are characterized by the presence of an excess of silica in the composition of the mixture.

Many glazes are formed by the use of basic frits. A frit is melted or compounded glass and its purpose is to permit the use of certain soluble ingredients in the glaze formula. Such materials as borax, boric acid and soda ash must be made insoluble before they are used. This is done by fritting them—that is, heating them to their molten state. This mass is then dripped into cold water. Upon touching the water the molten drops explode into crystals, which are then pulverized into a fine powder. Fritting is useful in making glazes that give crackle finishes, icelike finishes or bubble effects. In describing the method for making frits, it is necessary to oversimplify. The process requires a goodly amount of know-how and technical experience. This, plus the lack of necessary equipment, means that the beginner is better off buying commercially prepared frits from his supplier.

Lead glazes are most generally used by beginners because they are easy to apply, fire at a low temperature, and form a durable surface. They offer the common range of colors, but have a yellowish tinge and are not as brilliant as boracic or alkaline glazes, which offer such colors as turquoise, Persian blue, and cherry red. The latter are, however, more difficult to apply. Lead glazes may be purchased from any ceramic house, but as each firm names or numbers its glazes differently, you should order them according to the description or sample shown in the catalogue of a specific ceramics house.

Commercial glazes come in powder form. You will have to mix them with water. Since most glazes contain toxic materials, you should take precautions against breathing in the dust and avoid prolonged

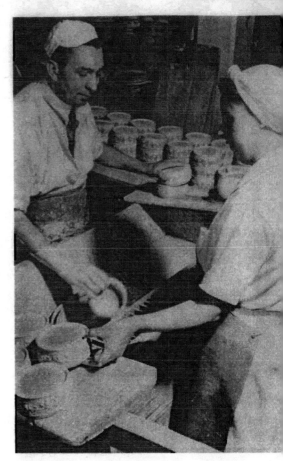

Wedgwood ware from biscuit oven is dipped in liquid glaze which has consistency of cream. Water in glaze is absorbed by ware, leaving glaze film.

contact with the skin, particularly where the skin may be broken.

Usually 65 cubic centimeters of water to 100 grams of glaze will give the consistency of heavy cream. The necessary consistency varies according to the ingredients of the glaze, the porosity of the piece to which it is applied, and the method of application. Experimenting with combinations and variations will provide interesting results.

To make a practical transparent glaze, use nine parts Frit No. G24 (manufactured by The O. Hommel Co., Box 475, Pittsburgh, Pa.), one part Georgia kaolin. To this mixture add about 2% ordinary borax to aid the glaze in flowing more evenly when fired. This glaze should be fired at about 1800 or 1900 degrees Fahrenheit.

In order to color this clear glaze, you may add stains in proportion to the depth

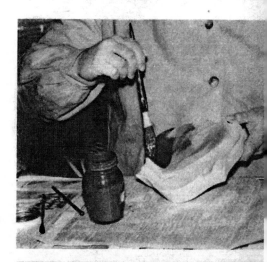

Glaze should be flowed on piece, and not brushed on or brush marks will appear; it is necessary to maintain an even coating or thickness of glaze, particularly when contrasting glaze is used over underglaze.

When brushing glaze over a large area it often is necessary to dry-foot the piece being glazed, in order to keep the glaze on the ceramic item from making contact with the kiln shelves. This also allows you to do away with unsightly stilt marks.

Photos from "Craftsmanship in Clay"

Shown above is most accepted method of glazing interior of ceramic piece. Pour your glaze into the piece and be careful to rotate the piece as you pour back into the container, to cover all areas.

of the color you desire, usually between 2% to 20% by weight. Glazes may also be tinted by the addition of underglaze colors, grinding them together while they are in a dry, powder state. The beginner, however, will find it much easier to use liquid stains, for two reasons—they are already milled and can be quickly mixed merely by stirring into the glaze. Most supply firms carry a wide range of such stains, enabling the hobbyist to develop his own distinctive colors.

A white glaze or white stain will render all of these glazes opaque. Should the glaze be colored, the addition of an opaquifier will not cause a radical color change in the finished ware. However, additional stain may have to be added to maintain the precise shade you are seeking. About 10% white will be enough to add to clear or colored glaze to render it opaque.

If you want a blue glaze it will be alkaline. To mix a typical glaze, take 64 parts soda ash, 30 parts whiting, 56 parts feldspar and 42 parts silica. Mix thoroughly by milling either with a mortar and pestle or with a ball mill. A ball mill consists of a porcelain jar which is set in a frame and made to revolve on its axis in a horizontal position. It is about half-filled with porcelain

or carborundum balls, which roll against each other and the walls of the jar and thereby do the milling.

You should weigh the ingredients, grind them in a dry state. Then mix just the quantity you need with water, because any that is left over will have to be discarded. Store the excess powder glaze dry. Stir in the water vigorously so the soda ash, which is soluble, will not harden. If it does, it will be difficult to break up. Do not add too much water because of the soluble ingredients. Remember that excess water cannot be poured off, since some of the ingredients would also pour off. Have the exact amount of water you require, otherwise the mixture may be spoiled and you will have to mix the glaze anew.

Now, by adding 4 to 5% black oxide of copper, you will get a beautiful turquoise blue. By reducing the amount of this oxide to 2 to 4%, an Egyptian blue will result. About ½% of black oxide of cobalt will bring about a rich sapphire tone. For opaque colors mix in 6 to 8% tin oxide.

Always screen a glaze thoroughly before applying it to a ware. A binder is necessary when the glaze is going to be used on bisque to prevent it from fluffing or chipping off. Binders are organic materials

Above, bowl is being glazed with spray gun. See that glaze is free-flowing, thin enough to spray easily through nozzle. Always test distance on piece of paper for best and even glaze coverage with spray. Spray booth is used, and mouth and nose should be masked. If you don't want to dry-foot the piece, use metal or ceramic stilt shown.

such as glue, gum tragacanth, dextrine or gelatine. Binders also help to hold the glaze in a colloidal or suspended state. But other ingredients are usually used for this purpose. These include calcium chloride, setit powder and bentonite. Only very small quantities should be used.

A properly prepared glaze is neither too thick nor too thin. If applied to a porous bisque surface, the glaze should be thinner than normal. This is because the water will be sucked out of the glaze very fast, leaving a thick coating deposited on the surface. If bisque is hard-fired, on the other hand, the glaze must be thicker than usual. Practice will teach you how much water should be added or poured off. If you need to thicken the glaze by pouring off some of the water, let it settle first for an hour or two and pour off the water at the top. There is little danger of losing any of the ingredients in the glaze by pouring off this water, since none of the ingredients are oluble and thus will sink to the bottom. Alkaline glazes, as already explained, are an exception to this rule.

It would take a book of many pages to cover all the processes, results, defects and cures encountered with glazes. Only the salient points have been touched upon here. Although the hobbyist who prepares his own glazes should be commended, the beginner is much better off buying commercial glazes at first. This does not mean that after you have learned the basic techniques, you should not go on and develop your own glazes. First, however, it is wise to obtain instruction from a professional ceramist who will aid you in perfecting your glazing methods.

Ceramic spray booth manufactured by Craftools, Inc., is 2 feet wide, comes complete with motor exhaust, turntable, stand and brackets for gun.

Applying the Glaze

After you have prepared your glaze and it is ready for use, you must decide upon a method for applying it. It is important to remember that when you glaze a piece you are coating the clay with powdered glass ingredients suspended in water. Color will appear only where it is applied. It is true that glazes flow out to even themselves as they melt and fuse to the clay body in the kiln, but they will not necessarily flow over a bare spot to hide it fully.

There are three main methods for applying glaze to a ware: dipping, spraying and brushing. Dipping is generally used by the studio where a large number of decorated bisque items are to be glazed and fired. The glaze is generally purchased in bulk in dry form. Water is added according to the manufacturer's instructions. Once the proper weight of liquid glaze is ascertained, it should be checked before each day's use and water added if necessary. For example, it has been found that a mixture of liquid glaze weighing about 22 ounces per pint is approximately the right consistency for the average piece to be fired at temperatures between 2174 degrees and 2246 degrees Fahrenheit.

Glaze gum is sometimes added to toughen the unfired glaze to facilitate handling. The glaze you purchase may already contain gum. If you are not sure, ask your supplier whether gum has been added. If additional gum is subsequently added to an excess, drying is considerably retarded and much time is lost before the piece can be handled and fired.

Dipping processes are many and varied. Some pieces, such as figurines, are often glazed only on the outside. The piece is simply held at the base by the most convenient grip and immersed headfirst in the glaze. It is advisable to have a dipping container large enough to permit a sweeping motion so that the piece can also be brought out headfirst, which causes the excess glaze to drain toward the bottom of the piece. This will eliminate drops or bumps of glaze on the upper part of the figurine, which ordinarily would require smoothing before firing. The spots where the piece was gripped are then touched up with a brush.

Vases, cups, bowls, etc., which require glaze inside and out call for a slightly different method. Some ceramists prefer to pour glaze on the inside, filling the piece and emptying it in rapid motion. This is allowed to dry and then the outside is dipped to the top edge to complete coverage. Others prefer to accomplish the glazing in one operation. By placing your thumb on the top lip of the object and one or two fingers on the base, the piece may be immersed in a sweeping motion, making sure the entire inside surface contacts the glaze, and brought out in a reverse motion. As in all processes, practice will determine the best-suited method for you.

Although there are inexpensive spray guns obtainable on today's market, a minority of hobbyists have the necessary equipment for glazing by this method. A spray booth, homemade or otherwise, is required so that the excess glaze may be recovered. A protective respirator should be worn since the glaze spray is readily inhaled and can be harmful to the lungs.

Even coverage of the piece and proper thickness of the applied glaze is not as easily controlled as it is by dipping. The glaze should be thinner in consistency so that it will readily pass through the spray-gun nozzle. To learn how to glaze with a spray gun, it is recommended that you get first-hand instruction. It is almost a "must" where spraying is concerned. Some hobbyists have utilized hand-pumped insecticide guns for this glazing purpose. Try it if you wish, but work out-of-doors in order to disperse the harmful fumes. The glaze solution should be as thin as milk. Pour it into the barrel of the insecticide gun and spray the entire piece with at least three coats. Since there are so many variables involved in any form of spray-glazing, this method is not recommended for tyros.

Applying glaze with a brush is generally used with colored glazes where unusual decorative results are desired.

The recent general trend has been toward the use of one-fire glazes. These can be bought in liquid, ready-to-use form at most supply houses. The term "one-fire" applies to the process of putting glaze on the unfired clay piece, letting it dry, and then firing only once. Brushing has thus come into prominence as a glazing method for the hobbyist. Beautifully decorated objects can be produced with brushes and one-fire glazes without requiring an extraordinary artistic talent.

The method of brushing glaze is easy. The first coat should be "drawn out," that is, actually brushed out—much like applying a primer coat when painting a house. A minimum of two coats is usually required. The second and successive coats are "laid on." This means the brush should be well filled with the prepared glaze, which is permitted to flow onto the piece without excessive pressure on the brush.

The number of coats which should be applied depends on the depth of the color desired. Also, the individual's idea of a coat must be considered. One person's three-coat coverage might well be as thick as another's five-coat application. Many beautiful and unusual effects can be obtained by using various color combinations side by side which may flow together, and by brushing one color over another.

With the typical piece of glazed ware, you should not glaze the underside. At least it should have an unglazed footing. If the footing has been covered with glaze, which is probable if it has been dipped, you can remove the glaze with a piece of fine sandpaper after the glaze has dried, but before

Once you've gotten into glazing you'll find that orderliness helps. Store glazes on shelves, separating flowing, crackle, underglaze, matte, etc.

Photographs on this page illustrate a variety of kiln firing errors. In the pitcher photo you see a mottled appearance made by bubbling during the firing; cause was too-thick application of glaze. Elephant above was correctly glazed in red but was overfired, thus causing the red to fire out in some places; it's a beautiful piece that everyone wants to make, but the question is: how much was it overfired? Vase is marred due to using flowing instead of regular glaze; painted part became covered.

it has been fired. This process is called *dry-footing.*

Glazes, in and of themselves, their choice and application, involve a complicated chemical change. There are many variations and their behavior is sometimes erratic, although much of the guesswork has been removed for hobbyists in recent years by ceramic engineers. The best advice is to restrain your expectations until you see the results. Constantly experiment and keep careful records of the experiments. Be alert to new and different qualities as they appear.

Glaze Defects

There are several common and recurring defects which you should recognize in glazes and be able to correct. These include crazing, crawling, flowing, peeling.

Crazing is the appearance of small cracks throughout the glaze. It is caused by the glaze contracting more than the clay in cooling. This is the main reason for combining only glazes and clays which have been designed for each other. Crazing effects are not desirable for utilitarian pottery because water and food juices would seep through the cracks.

Craftools photo

Important for the ceramist who wishes to experiment seriously with glazes is the ball mill, a device that revolves and causes porcelain jars containing powdered glazes and flint pebbles to turn continuously, thus thoroughly mixing glaze.

However, there is a decorative technique, called *crackling*, by which the glaze is crazed purposefully by the ceramist. In fact, oil paint or India ink is often rubbed into the surface to accentuate the cracks. This type of glazing is reserved for sculpture or such objects as cigarette boxes, banks, etc., which need not be impervious to water or food.

A glaze is said to "crawl" when it pulls away from the body in small areas and exposes the clay. Refiring to a higher temperature, or applying a second coat of glaze with the addition of a flux, such as feldspar, and firing again will sometimes remedy crawling.

If a glaze is fired beyond the temperature for which it was intended, it may flow off the piece. Low percentages of flint or china clay added to the glaze will stiffen it and prevent flowing. But it is much wiser to fire a glaze precisely at the right temperature and not take the gamble of compensating for error.

Either the glaze, or possibly the glaze and decorative slip, may peel or break from the surface of the piece. One cause may be a too-thick application of slip, or applying slip on ware that is too dry. •

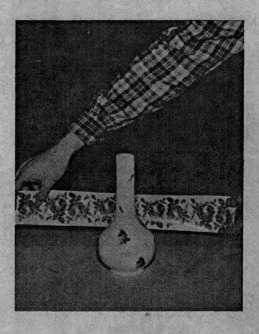

Decals that can be applied over or under some glazes are available. Shown here is strip of decals behind a piece to which some are already added.

kilns

Choose your kiln to suit the kind of ceramics you'll do, and learn how to use it for maximum performance.

KILNS have been used by man for many thousands of years. Excavations of ancient sites of early civilizations indicate that the most primitive kilns were of the updraft type. In most cases, they consisted only of a firing chamber, a perforated floor and a wall. The construction of a permanent kiln was too much of a structural problem for early potters. Recourse was made to a temporary roof of green poles and raw clay which would hold together long enough for the very low firing temperatures used at that time.

The modern kiln has vast improvements over the primitive types. However, the four main essentials which must be present in all kilns have not changed. There must be a means for producing heat, a support for the ware to be fired, a wall to contain the heat, and a means for transferring the heat from its source to the ware.

Firing a piece of ceramic ware is generally the final step. It is also the most necessary. If a piece is not fired properly, all the work that has gone before is lost. Many types of kilns—or heat-treating ovens—are in use today. Most common in home workshops is the periodic kiln, which has a complete cycle from cold to warm to hot to cold. By contrast, in large commercial potteries, the kilns maintain a constant heat and the ware is passed through them on conveyer belts or flatcars at a predetermined speed.

When you place a piece of dough with yeast in your kitchen oven, the heat causes certain chemical changes which result in a loaf of bread. A periodic kiln can be likened to your kitchen oven, the only important difference being its ability to attain much hotter temperatures which likewise cause certain chemical changes in clay and glazes. Most kilns are constructed of refractory bricks or tiles for inner walls. These walls are insulated in order to keep the heat evenly distributed throughout firing chamber. This is of utmost importance and by no means easy to achieve. In fact, few large periodic kilns show a difference of less han 50 degrees Fahrenheit from top to bottom.

Another advantage of insulation is that it reduces the amount of fuel necessary to reach the desired temperature. Some kilns, particularly those in commercial potteries, are heated with gas or oil fuels. Electricity, however, is much more practical for the hobbyist, since it is much easier to control, extremely flexible and available at reasonable cost in most parts of the United States and Canada. The studio with a gas- or oil-burning kiln is rare nowadays.

The main shortcoming of an electric kiln is that the atmosphere in the firing chamber cannot be controlled. In some rare instances the professional ceramist may want a reducing atmosphere rather than the ordinary oxidizing condition. A reduction flame firing will have to be made in a gas or oil kiln, if one can be found nearby.

Before choosing a kiln for your studio, you must take into consideration the amount of electricity you have available. If only normal electricity for lighting is available, then your kiln size or firing area is limited to just that power.

Also important to consider is heat loss. Obviously it requires more power to heat a large kiln than a small one to the same temperature. The main principle involved in firing a kiln is that the outlet is smaller than the inlet, so that there will always be pressure. Without this pressure, it would be impossible to build up high temperatures in the kiln.

Hence, a kiln chamber must be confined, and heavily insulated as well, in order to prevent too great a heat loss. It follows, too, that the more power available, the larger the kiln interior can be, and many more pieces can be fired at one time.

Finally, you must consider how you want to load the kiln for firing. You can choose between a front-door opening, or one which is loaded from the top. This is pretty much a matter of personal preference. A little experience loading both types will decide the question for you.

Many people, interested in trying their hand at making pottery, become discouraged when the cost of firing equipment is learned. Yet, to leave a piece unfired or to depend upon someone else's skill is shirking, for the firing of a piece is the real test of its structural and decorative merit.

Though the initial outlay for a kiln can be fairly expensive, the actual cost is low. Properly used and maintained, the life span of a well-made kiln can be measured in generations. Considering the importance of a kiln to any studio and the many years of service it is capable of giving, a kiln is a prudent investment if it is purchased wisely. Remember, however, that even the best kiln improperly used can be reduced to a machine of ugly disappointments within a short time.

The beginner is advised against firing his own pieces until he has had some instruction in the use of a kiln. An exception may be made, though, in the firing of jewelry, small tiles and small pieces cast in a mold. This is because small electric kilns for this type of firing can be purchased for as little as $35 to $50 today. Thus the beginner is

Below left, the author's son has removed plug from the spy-hole to see if proper firing has been reached, as determined by position of cone. Plugs are put in only after moisture has escaped, when pyrometer shows about 500°F. Right, switches on face of top-loading kiln are for three heat levels.

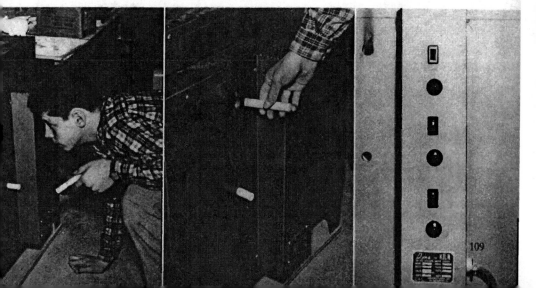

Shelves having glaze drippings on them from previous firings must be cleaned to prevent glaze from sticking to next batch fired. Chisel off glaze, then cover what remains with kiln wash, applying in a milky-thin mixture made by adding water to kiln-wash powder. Use paint brush; brush hairs that adhere to shelves will fire out. Too heavy wash may peel or adhere to piece resting on it during firing. Apply kiln wash only to side of shelf that is to support wares; do not reverse shelves in the kiln—always keep same side up, or kiln wash may fall on ware on lower shelf during the firing.

not forced to pay out large sums of money until he is certain he can and wants to operate a larger kiln. Because of the rapid rise in temperature in a test kiln, as these small models are called, only thin objects no more than one-quarter inch in thickness should be fired. Any object thicker than that may explode in the kiln.

Many ambitious ceramists have constructed their own kilns. Unless you are an accomplished builder, however, it is advisable to buy a ready-made kiln. No matter how fine a set of instructions for building a kiln one uses, some problems almost always arise. Often one has to hunt for a long time before he determines the cause of the difficulty and eliminates them; sometimes the advice of an expert is necessary. Such delays and worries are discouraging to the beginner. The majority of hobbyists who have built their own kilns will readily admit the finished product was not worth the effort. Almost without exception, the homemade kiln is less dependable than the factory-produced kiln.

One word of caution, however—always check the reputation of a kiln manufacturer before buying. There have been some shoddy models put on the market in the past and some unwary buyers learned to their regret that they had been bilked. When you buy a kiln, make certain it is the best available at the price you wish to pay. Compare competing lines. Do not hesitate to ask for the advice of another ceramist who is qualified to give counsel. Larger kilns are heavy and costly to ship, so if possible try to select one that is manufactured in your section of the country.

The cost of a kiln is also determined largely by the temperature it is capable of attaining. A small test kiln, such as that recommended for firing tile and jewelry, can reach 1800 degrees Fahrenheit in one or two hours. Larger kilns will take longer to get this hot. However, if a higher temperature is desired, only a larger kiln can give it to you.

A good all-around kiln will be able to deliver up to approximately 2300 degrees Fahrenheit in a reasonable length of time. There are kilns which go higher, of course, but the price begins to rise in a geometric proportion to the amount of heat which can be had in these high-fire kilns. For most purposes, 2300 degrees Fahrenheit is sufficient. Fine, hard-paste porcelain, for example, can be fired at this temperature.

Before you fire any ware, naturally you must know the maturing points of both the clay and the glaze. You must know at what temperature the ware will collapse, vitrify, or melt. Otherwise, how would you know when to shut off the kiln? Time or duration of fire depends a great deal on weather conditions, weight of the ware in the kiln, or mass. Thus, while the time factor is important, it is not sufficiently accurate.

A thermometer is useless at the high temperatures attained in a kiln. Most thermometer liquids would boil if exposed to such intense heat, and the container for such liquid would surely melt.

This situation resulted in the development of the pyrometer. It is an old principle of physics that certain dissimilar metals, twisted together and welded at the end, will develop small amounts of eletricity when subjected to heat. The ratio of electricity increases with the amount of heat. The amount of electricity can be recorded on a microvoltameter. This is calibrated and charted in terms of degrees, permitting you to read the temperature inside the firing chamber.

Another method of determining temperature is by the use of cones. These are small pyramid-shaped pieces of clay, which will melt at a predetermined temperature. Most electric kilns have spyholes cut in the front of the kiln with a removable plug. The cone is placed inside the kiln so that it can be seen through the spy-hole.

Each cone has a number on it. When you observe the cone beginning to bend inside the kiln, the temperature denoted by the number on the cone has been reached and the kiln is shut off. The use of cones is quite an accurate means for gauging temperature. Cones are often employed as a check against the pyrometer.

This method of measuring kiln heat has become so universal that maturing temperatures are more often than not given in terms of cone numbers. (See chart of temperature equivalents of pyrometric cones in this chapter.) For example, if you used a clay which matures at Cone 8, you would know that the equivalent in Fahrenheit degrees is roughly 2250. Likewise, a glaze which fuses properly at Cone 08 would require a temperature of about 1733 degrees Fahrenheit.

In the first instance, you would place a cone bearing the number 8 in the kiln and wait until it bends before shutting off the kiln. In the second instance, you would use a cone numbered 08 and wait for it to bend before shutting off the kiln.

There is, as you have seen, a large difference between Cone 8 and Cone 08. The numbering of cones begins at 022, equivalent to 1085 degrees Fahrenheit, and continues up to 20, equivalent to 2770 degrees Fahrenheit. When there is a zero in front of the number, the equivalent temperature rises as the number *decreases*. When there is no zero before the number, the temperature continues to rise as the number *increases*. (See chart of equivalents.)

Many ceramists employ another check on the accuracy of cones. Instead of using a single cone, they line up three in full sight through the spy-hole. Suppose they are firing a ware which matures at Cone 06. Then they would place one 05 cone, one 06 cone and one 07 cone in the kiln. When the 05 and 06 cones have bent, but before the 07 cone has started to bend, they will shut

Cracks in bottom of kiln will allow heat escape from this area and affect your ware; see below.

Vacuum out bottom, mix bonding cement in plastic bowl and fill in cracks or depressions in kiln.

Smooth, workable mixture of bonding cement was applied and sanded. Cover lightly with kiln wash.

Left are shown cones used to determine firing temperature. Usually you place three cones in kiln, unless you have a pyrometer. To fire at Cone 6, you place Cones 5, 6 and 7 in the kiln at eye level. When Cone 5 bends, that's the signal that you're approaching desired temperature; if you wait too long and Cone 7 bends, you've overfired. Above, the straight cone is bent as shown when you shut off kiln.

TEMPERATURE EQUIVALENTS
ORTON STANDARD PYROMETRIC CONES

CONE NUMBER	LARGE CONES	SMALL CONES	CONE NUMBER	LARGE CONES	SMALL CONES
Heated at:	270° F.	540° F.	Heated at:	270° F.	540° F.
022	1112	1121*	06	1830	1873
021	1137	1189	05	1915	1944
020	1175	1231	04	1940	2008
019	1261	1333	03	2014	2068
018	1323	1386	02	2048	2098
017	1377	1443	01	2079	2152
016	1458	1517	1	2109	2154
015	1479	1549	2	2124	2154
014	1540	1526*	3	2134	2185
013	1566	1580*	4	2167	2208
012	1623	1607*	5	2185	2230
011	1641	1661*	6	2232	2291
010	1641	1686	7	2264	2301
09	1693	1751	8	2305	2372
08	1751	1801	9	2336	2403
07	1803	1846	10	2381	2426

* Temperature equivalents shown for these cones were not determined in tests. Values given have been estimated for your convenience.

COLOR SCALE FOR TEMPERATURES

COLOR	APPX. CONE	DEGREES F.
Lowest visible red to dark red	022 to 019	885 to 1200
Dark red to cherry red	018 to 016	1200 to 1380
Cherry red to bright cherry red	015 to 014	1380 to 1500
Bright Cherry red to orange	013 to 010	1500 to 1650
Orange to Yellow	09 to 03	1650 to 2000
Yellow to light yellow	02 to 10	2000 to 2400

Pyrometer is used to determine approximate temperature in kiln; for accuracy, cone must be used.

off the kiln. If only the 05 cone has bent, the kiln has not reached the maturing point. If all three cones have bent, the ware has been overfired.

The use of cones and pyrometers requires the attendance of the kiln operator, who must be on hand to shut the kiln off when the proper temperature has been reached. This has been overcome recently with the introduction of thermostatic controls which automatically snap off the kiln at the desired temperature.

One such device is called the Kiln-gard. It is patented and sold by dealers throughout North America. It consists of two projecting fingers, spring-loaded and held apart by a pyrometric cone. These fingers are inserted through the spy-hole in the kiln. When the cone melts in the firing chamber, the fingers close, shutting off a switch which in turn snaps off the kiln's source of electricity.

Small enameling kiln by the L&L Manufacturing Co. reflects the current craze for copper jewelry with ceramic glaze. Below is large-capacity Paragon kiln.

There are simple rules to follow in the care and maintenance of kilns to obtain properly fired ware, uninterrupted production and a long kiln life with a minimum of repair.

1. Do not overfire. If you do not know the normal safe temperature ceiling for your kiln, write to the company that manufactured it. The firm will be glad to furnish this and any other information about the kiln.

2. Do not overload. Get circulation throughout. Set all ware so that heat may pass freely through the firing chamber. It is a temptation to load a kiln too tightly, especially when the ware consists of small pieces.

3. Replace damaged parts. Wear invites wear. Faulty parts almost always cause poor results in the firing.

Model H-145 hobbyist kiln made by D.H.C. Kilns, Inc., measures 13 inches high, has maximum temperature of 2000°F; around $65.

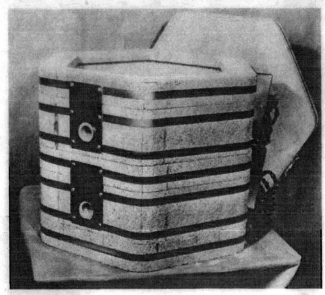

D.H.C. porcelain kiln, below, stands 29 inches high and costs about $124. Its maximum heat is 2400°F; case is of welded steel.

Model TL-6 top-loading kiln made by Harrop Ceramic Service Co. sells for about $100 crated (prices given on all kilns is with crating). Height is 20 inches. Switch has three heat speeds. Harrop bench-model kiln is shown at the beginning of chapter, has a pyrometer.

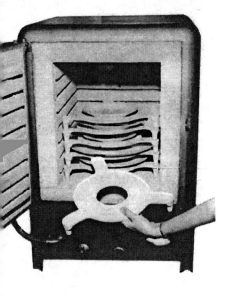

Model SF-2 front-loading kiln is 56 inches high, comes with pyrometer, pilot lights and other features (bottom stand not shown in photo) for $390; it's made by Paragon Industries, Inc.

L&L Model 424 front-loading kiln above heats to 2300°F, is fine for studio; cost, over $1000. Manufacturer makes various kiln types, sizes.

4. Do not rush the firing. Building up the temperature gradually during early stages avoids excessive strain on both the ware and the kiln.

5. The kiln should be kept free of dust at all times. Should any foreign matter reach a heating element in an electric kiln, it should be carefully removed before firing.

6. If small cracks appear on the inside walls, leave them alone. These cracks are inherent with insulating firebrick. They are not harmful in any way, since they close when the kiln is heated, due to the expansion of the material. It is the same principle as the expansion joints in sidewalks, highways and bridges.

7. Kiln wash should be used on the tops of shelves and on the kiln floor before firing ceramic glazes. It is painted on with a brush and usually consists of one-half kaolin and one-half water, mixed with water to the consistency of light cream. Kiln wash is used to prevent glaze drippings from sticking to the shelf or the kiln floor. It is not generally recommended to use kiln wash on the kiln walls.

8. Be certain that your electrical service is capable of delivering sufficient power for the kiln. Do not overload the circuit. It is wiser to install a new service which de-

livers more power. Your local power and light company, or your electrician, will be able to advise you on the service your kiln requires.

9. Electrical connections in the kiln may in time become loose due to the effect of expansion and contraction. At any sign of excessive heat at the plug or at the terminal of the kiln, the connection should be examined. If severe blacking of the copper wire is noted, this should be sanded bright, and a new connection made.

10. Should at any time a heating element begin to come out of the grooves, place a heating element staple at the center of the bulge and very carefully push it into the brick wall of the kiln. Caution must be used when handling the elements after they have been heated and cooled. After the staple is in place, fire the kiln to at least Cone 06 to soften the element and allow it to take a new set.

In the event that the heating element has moved entirely out of the groove before maintenance is attempted, do not try to put all the element back at once. With a staple, move it part of the way toward the groove, fire the kiln, then push the staple to a better position and fire the kiln again. Repeat as many times as necessary until the element is back in the proper place. •

115

firing the ware

Success or failure? It's a suspenseful moment when you open the kiln door.

IN THE ENTIRE field of ceramic art there is no greater thrill for either the amateur or the professional than to open the door of the kiln on a perfectly fired "load" of either bisque or glazed ware. By the same token, there is no greater heartbreak than to open the door on a poorly fired "load."

All ware must be absolutely dry before it is fired. The most important item that goes into your kiln is the cone. Pyrometric cones measure *heat work* due to effect of time, temperature and atmosphere. The degree of maturity in a fired clay body, within limits, is likewise controlled by time, temperature and atmosphere. A cone should not be considered simply as a temperature measuring device such as a pyrometer. Important: When cones are heated at different rates of heat rise they have different deformation temperatures.

The cones should be set in place at a slight angle of about 8 degrees to the vertical. Ceramic clay may be used to hold cones 022 through 04. Set the cone in a tiny pat of clay so that the number of the cone is not imbedded and the cone is slightly tilted. When clay is used as a cone support, allow it to dry at room temperature before placing the cone in the kiln, or it might explode during the firing.

Using the face of a clock perhaps is the best way to illustrate the degree of tilt and the proper cone position when the firing is completed. When the cone is mounted in the clay, it should tilt at about the one o'clock position. When the cone has bent in the firing to the three o'clock position, your kiln should be turned off.

Your supply house for ceramic materials will be glad to recommend the proper cone number to be used when firing a given material. Always fire ware to the hottest cone first. For example, if you use an 05 body and an 08 glaze—regardless of whether the glaze is suitable for one firing with a body you are not using—you must fire your greenware to an 05 bisque fire to mature the clay before you apply the 08 glaze.

If a clay body is hardened in the kiln before glaze is applied, it is said to have been bisque-fired. When a glazed piece is baked in the kiln it is said to have been glost-fired. There are several distinct differences between these two types of firing, particularly in the way the kiln is loaded.

Various sizes of shelves, posts and stilts, known as kiln furniture, are necessary for stacking both a bisque and glaze fire. T posts are used to support the shelves. using taller or shorter posts you will able to raise, lower or increase the numb of shelves in the firing chamber.

All kiln furniture is made of refracto materials which are impervious to the hi kiln temperatures. Usually these he resistant pieces are cut from the same ty of insulating brick used in making yo kiln. When exposed to heat, your k furniture should not crack, split or melt

It is a basic law of physics that hot always rises; cool air always sinks. Th the lower half of your kiln is always coo than the top. This makes it necessary, wh loading a bisque fire, to place the heavi thicker pieces on the bottom or cooler ar of the kiln. These pieces are more like to be ruined by sudden changes in tei perature than are the thinner wares.

Try to arrange the shelves economica in the kiln so that you can fire as mu greenware as possible. In a bisque firi the pieces may touch each other and r directly on the shelf or floor of the ki They should, however, be kept at least o inch away from the heating elements of electric kiln. It is not a good practice stack ware on top of or inside other wa because the weight is liable to shatter t bottom pieces. The ware can be stacked its side if done with care. If a piece has cover, such as a cigarette box, it should fired in place on top of the main body.

All sizes of shelves and supports are used in a kiln, and can be bought to suit your kiln size.

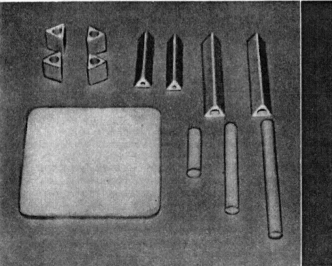

Below is shown how the shelves are supported posts inside kiln. See photos on following pag

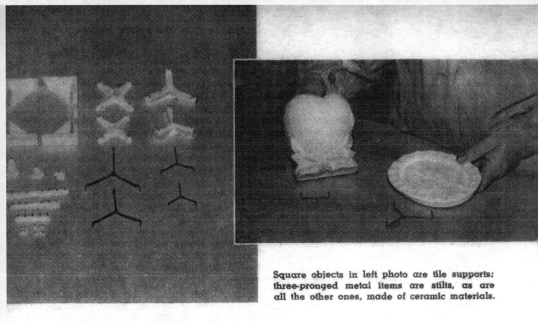

Square objects in left photo are tile supports; three-pronged metal items are stilts, as are all the other ones, made of ceramic materials.

Generally speaking, sculptured pieces are stacked separately. The chance of such a piece chipping or breaking in the kiln is greater and this may destroy other ware in the kiln. Before it is fired, a piece of sculpture should have a minimum drying time of six weeks. Remember it must be hollow or be constructed around an armature which will be oxidized by the kiln heat. Otherwise an uneven distribution of heat through the body of the ware will almost certainly cause it to collapse or, worse, explode.

Sculpture is often considered finished in the bisque state, particularly when executed in terra cotta or sculpture clays. Pottery must have a glaze finishing, at least on the inside, to make it usable and easy to clean. Furthermore, the color of many pottery clays is innocuous and uninteresting as ordinary bisque. The color and texture of glaze are necessary to give it esthetic quality.

Place as much heavy ware on the floor of the kiln as you can, leaving room in the corners for four posts which are about one inch taller than the tallest piece of greenware. If the kiln is hexagonal, the shelves will be hexagonal or round, and three stilts should be used for support. The posts, of course, should be the same height in order to hold the shelf perfectly level. Gently lower the shelf in place atop the supports. Stack more ware on the shelf. You may stack up as many shelves as you need or space permits. Place the cones on one shelf, where it can be clearly seen through the spy-hole in the front of the kiln.

The ware should be stacked in such a manner that the hot air can circulate freely through the kiln. Passages of a couple of inches should be left open from the top to the bottom of the kiln and from side to side to give the kiln a chance to heat evenly. Otherwise, some of the ware will come out hard and properly matured and some will come out soft and have to be refired.

A kiln which loads through a front door affords a better view of shelf clearance, but not as much assurance with respect to the space between pieces of ware being fired. The opposite is true of the top-loader.

What chemical changes take place in the kiln when you have begun the bisque firing process? First you should know that no matter how dry the greenware appears when you put it into the kiln, there is always a minute quantity of chemical moisture present. This moisture is known as *water smoke*. And it must be eliminated, after which the clay loses forever its plasticity.

You should start bisque firing at a relatively low heat. Keep the temperature at about 500 to 600 degrees Fahrenheit for an hour or two. If possible, keep the kiln door slightly ajar during this period to permit free escape of the chemical moisture in the clayware. This period of firing is called water-smoking or "water out." If the heat were increased too rapidly at the start, the moisture would turn to steam and would blow up the stacked ware in the kiln. Even after you close the door, leave the spy-hole open until the inside of the firing chamber begins to glow red from the heat. The open spy-hole will act as a vent for water smoke.

By holding a mirror to the spy-hole, you can check to see if water smoke is still be-

Photos above and adjacent at left show the ware
about to be stilted and, second, on top of stilts.
Naturally, stilting process is done in the kiln.

ing baked from the ware. As long as there
is moisture escaping, the mirror will become steam-misted and there may be moisture around the spy-hole. When the mirror
does not become steamed, you will know
that all the moisture has been driven out.

When this happens, seal the kiln tightly.
Gradually increase the temperature until
the ware reaches its maturing point. The
heat should then be turned off and the
ware slowly cooled within the kiln. If you
are using a periodic electric kiln, the temperature will automatically rise as long as
the power is on. In other words, the longer
the power is on the hotter will become the
kiln. Periodically remove the plug from the
spy-hole and check the cone. When it is
properly bent, you know the maturing point
has been reached.

Do not open the kiln immediately after
turning off the power. A safe rule-of-
thumb is not to open the kiln until twice
the firing time has elapsed. Then you may
unplug the spy-hole and open the door no
more than an inch or so. When another hour
has passed, the door may be nudged open
about one-quarter of the way. Wait another
hour before removing the fired bisque from
the kiln.

Be cautious that you don't burn your
fingers. If you want to remove the ware
now, rather than letting it cool in the kiln
chamber, use heavy gloves or tongs. Place
the still-hot pieces on some fireproof material, such as Transite or asbestos. Never
set hot ware on paper or wood lest a fire
be started. Freshly fired bisque should be
kept out of drafts, since a quick temperature change may cause it to shatter. For
this reason you shouldn't use unheated

tongs to remove your ware from the kiln

The hardness of bisque ware which
comes out of the kiln can be tested by
scratching the base with a knife. This can
be done after the ware has cooled completely. If the knife cuts into the baked
clay, it is called *soft paste*. If it is difficult
to cut into the bisque and the knife leaves
a dark mark, it is called *hard paste*. The
hardness can also be judged by hitting the
bisque lightly with a nail. If it has a flat
sound, it is soft. If it has a bell-like ring
it is hard.

Hard-paste bisque has usually been fired
at a higher temperature than soft-paste. I
must be kept in mind that the higher the
fire, the more a piece shrinks, and thereby
becomes more dense and less porous. This
will make the glaze application somewhat
more difficult.

The stacking of a kiln for glaze, or glost
firing is more complicated than for bisque
firing. Much more care is needed when ar-
ranging a glaze kiln. Most important is that
none of the glaze pieces touch one another
nor touch the shelf or any part of the kiln
Glaze will flow when heated and will stick
to anything with which it comes in contact

Paint the floor of the kiln and the top
side of the shelves with kiln wash. (See
preceding chapter.) With many kilns it is
also necessary to brush kiln wash on the
walls. Prepared washes can be purchased
from supply houses, although this is hardly
necessary since it is so easy to prepare
yourself. The wash tends to seal these surfaces so particles of dirt, sand, clay, etc.
will not fall onto the ware and become
imbedded in the molten glaze. It is advisable before stacking the glazed ware in the
firing chamber to brush down the ceiling
and the walls of the kiln with an ordinary
whisk broom to remove all such foreign
particles. Many ceramists used a vacuum
cleaner to clean the interior of their kilns

In stacking ware for a glost fire, place
the thinner ware on the bottom of the kiln
just the reverse of the bisque fire. The
hottest area will provide the best soaking
position, since heavy ware will require
more heat soaking than the thin ware. Use
the kiln furniture as you did for bisque
firing. Load your kiln as economically as
possible, but do not expect to get as many
pieces of glazed ware in the chamber as
you did greenware. Each glazed piece
must be separated from the next piece and
from the shelf-supports by at least three
eighths of an inch.

If the piece is glazed on the bottom, it
must be supported on stilts. Otherwise it
will stick to the shelf or the kiln floor
Stilts are flat pieces of refractory brick or

le which have three or four wire points icking upward, upon which the ware is laced. Use the largest stilt available for ie piece being stacked so that it is perctly balanced. This is important, for if a ingle piece of glazed ware topples over uring the firing, it may start others falling ke the proverbial house of cards. Porceiin pieces are set directly on the kilnashed floor or shelf and are never placed n stilts.

Stilts are not necessary to support glazed are, if it has been dry-footed. To dryoot a piece of ware, remove all the glaze rom the part of the ware that will rest n the shelf or the floor of the kiln. The laze may be removed with a wet sponge, r a wet scrap of wool. Since no glaze will hus come into contact with shelf or kiln, o stilt is required. However, if the glaze s over-fired it is liable to flow to the botom of the ware and stick to the shelf or :iln floor.

Keeping each level of your kiln stacked vith pieces of similar height will enable ou to get the most out of your firing area. Vhen placing shelves in the kiln over :lazed ware, be certain that the underside f the shelf is clean. Dust or foreign matter n the underside of a shelf will drop on the vare below, stick to the glaze and cause lefects in the finished ware.

Glost firing need not be as gradual as »isque firing, since the clay has usually »een already fired and water-smoked. If, 1owever, you are firing glazed greenware, ollow the same procedure to remove :hemical moisture as you did for bisque iring.

To fire glazed bisque ware, use a low 1eat for about 20 minutes and let the door stand open for this time. Without closing he door, increase the heat to high. Wait 1nother 20 minutes before closing the door.

Be careful never to jar or shake the kiln during a glost firing. Otherwise, the pieces may fall from their delicate perches on the stilts and be spoiled. If a glazed piece is stacked so it overhangs a shelf, molten glaze is likely to drip off and ruin any ware below.

See that the heat is increased steadily and that it is not allowed to drop back at any time. If the firing does drop back at the time the glaze begins to melt, blisters and defects will form which will mar the finished ware.

Shut off the kiln at the proper maturing temperature, when the cone has bent to the three o'clock position. Do not open the kiln until it has completely cooled. A sudden draft of cold air will cause crazing on most glazeware. If a glaze has been underfired, it will look dull and lusterless. Too much heat will cause the glaze to run, leaving large areas of the surface bare and unglazed. An improperly fired piece can be glazed and fired again, but you will probably find it difficult to make the second coat of glaze stick to the once-glazed surface. As many as five coats are often required to get a heavy enough coverage for refiring.

This presents another problem. If glaze is applied too generously it may begin dripping from the ware when it is heated to the molten state. Upon cooling, this excess glaze usually is left hanging from the bottom of the ware, like miniature stalactites. These hangings must be removed with a file or a carborundum wheel. Take care always to grind in, toward the ware, lest the glaze be pulled from the surface in large chips.

Some colored glazes will "travel" in the firing if placed in the kiln with other unmatured glazes. This will result in a gray cast to an otherwise beautiful glaze. This

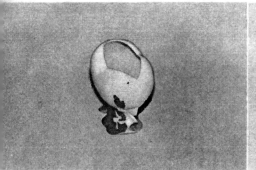

Crack occurred in finished ware in kiln due to small neglected crack that broadened in firing.

Improperly mended greenware led to whole section of repair separating from body of ware in firing.

phenomenon is caused by the gaseous chemicals forced from some glazes by the intense heat. These gases often affect the atmosphere in the firing chamber and bring about undesired chemical changes in other glazes they contact.

Should you happen to fire such a combination of glazes to produce this effect, note the colors fired together so that in the future you will fire these colors separately —unless, of course, you desire the gray tinge.

Overglaze decorations generally fire at a much lower temperature than glazes, since they are fired only to the softening point of the glaze over which they are applied. For this reason, the ware on which the overglaze decoration is applied affects the maturing point of the overglaze decoration.

All overglaze paints must be dry before being placed in the kiln. If this simple rule is not followed, you are likely to have trouble with the colors on the finished piece. Overglazed ware should be stacked the same as glazed ware. When you are doing a gold, china paint or luster firing it is necessary to leave the door of the kiln slightly open to allow the escape of the strong fumes which are generated by the oils evaporating and burning off as the heat rises. Although these fumes are annoying, they are quite harmless and proper ventilation will eliminate them.

Certain overglaze paints take less firing than others. All overglaze colors are not fired to the same cone even when placed on the same piece of ware. The colors to be fired to the hotter cone must be fired *before* the colors to be fired to the cooler cone are placed on the ware. Overglaze on a hard china piece must be fired to a hotter cone than the same overglaze applied to softer clay body.

It always pays to test your kiln by plac-

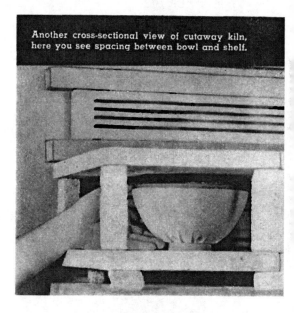

Another cross-sectional view of cutaway kiln, here you see spacing between bowl and shelf.

ing several cones at different spots in the firing chamber and thereby determining which are the cool and hot spots in your particular kiln. Always place the more sensitive overglaze paints in the coolest spots.

Not until you have mastered the technique of firing can you truly call yourself an accomplished ceramist. You are almost certain to have a number of failures and disappointments the first few times you operate your kiln. However, if you use the finest materials and equipment available, and if extreme care and cleanliness are used in firing your ware, you should not suffer too many disappointments. To get the most pleasure from your ceramic hobby, by all means learn how to use a kiln and do your own firing. •

how to pour a mold

Creating your own greenware saves money and gives added satisfaction. Here Gertrude Engel shows every step from pouring to finish.

SEVERAL molds, a gallon of slip (liquefied clay), a kitchen table to work on, a wooden mixing spoon and a crock or glass jar to pour from, a single wood modeling tool or an orange stick—and you are ready to turn out lovely ceramic bodies that, when finished, you can sell or give as presents.

The above materials will make the greenware that you can paint or glaze for a finished product. Today, manufacturers make varied and beautiful glazes that are easy to apply, and anyone can create ceramic pieces of fine appearance with little experience.

One thing to keep in mind when you use a brand-new mold is that the first couple of pieces to come out of the mold seldom are good. After that, the mold will be broken-in and turn out good ware. •

Photos in this chapter by Simon H

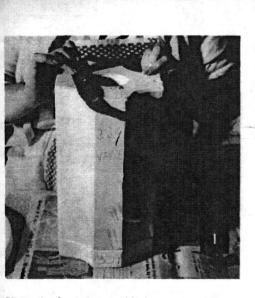

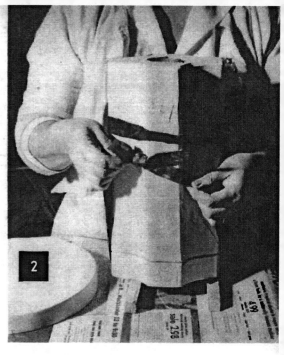

Above is three-piece mold that consists of two sides and bottom. When you buy a mold from a commercial house each piece has keys or notches that fit together correctly, so you can't vary the use. Molds don't come with rubber bands to hold them together during the molding process, so make your own; best bands are made from a tire inner tube.

Slide rubber band over width, another over length. Mold must be held together tightly, so add more bands if needed. Insufficient tightness will result in mess since slip will seep through crevice.

Left, finished piece is a beauty, and a credit to your work. After it was fired to its proper cone number, kiln was shut off; when thoroughly cooled, door was left ajar until most hot air and gases escaped and then opened completely. Do not remove ware until quite cool, to protect glaze.

Always spread newspapers down where you work for easy clean-up afterward. Once you open can of slip, which can be bought in one-gallon size, do not keep slip in can for longer than it takes to mix slip; otherwise, the slip will become tinged with rust stains. Keep slip in glass, ceramic or porcelain-lined container. Here, slip was poured into glass jar and mixed evenly and slowly with wooden spoon for about ten minutes, to a creamy liquid. Mixing too hard will create air bubbles.

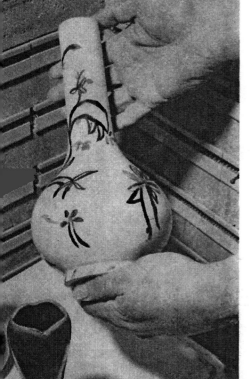

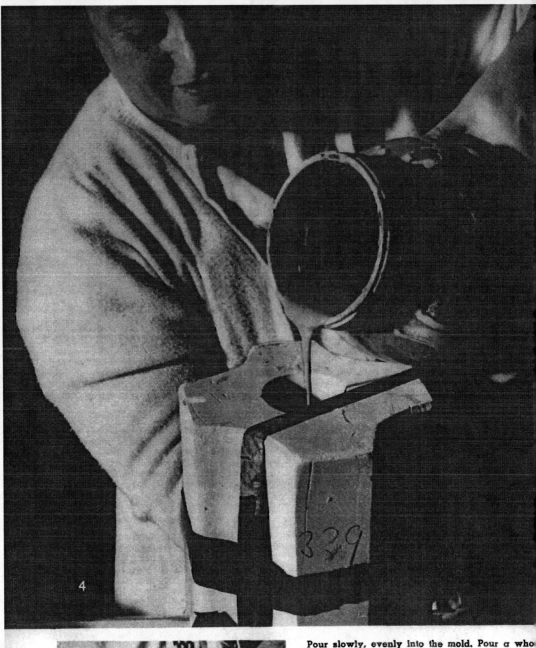

4

Pour slowly, evenly into the mold. Pour a who[le]
mold without stopping or lines will appear in th[e]
piece you are casting. Pour slowly to let all [air]
escape from the mold and insure fine detail wor[k.]

Time how long slip is kept in mold. Piece of th[is]
size usually needs to stand about 15 minutes f[or]
the first casting; add 2 minutes to time for ea[ch]
additional piece cast during continuous use, a[nd]
don't cast more than three or four at any on[e]
time or mold will get too wet and not opera[te]
properly. Plaster absorbs water from slip, allo[w-]
ing clay to coat mold; if slip settles, add mor[e]

5

Now pour out slip, back into container, and pour slowly to prevent piece from collapsing. Allow it to drain as you keep hand steadied on container.

Keep mold upside down and let it drain on newspaper; rest it on two sticks. Keep it there until slip (now clay) loses its shine and looks dull.

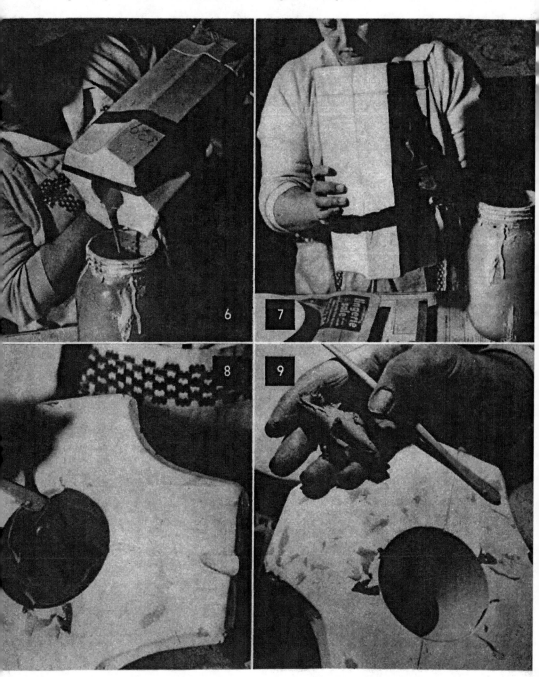

Turn mold over and with soft wooden modeling tool release the spare at top of mold. This is waste clay that is always at top of mold; discard it.

This is how mold looks with spare pulled off. Always use extreme care in working with tools on a mold since it's easy to gouge out bit of plaster.

Lift mold off the base and place it on a plaster bat. If piece you're casting is ready to come out of mold, the base will be released very easily.

Now separate the two sides, one at a time. Again, if the sides release easily the piece is ready to come out. If rushed, piece may collapse on bat.

Vase is placed on a bat, with three-piece mold alongside. Trim off excess clay where spare was, and set piece aside to dry, keeping it on bat.

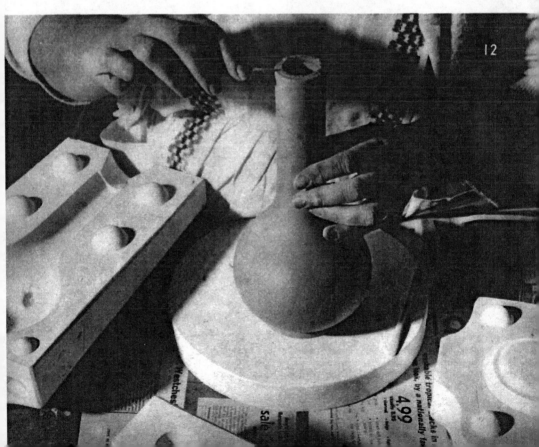

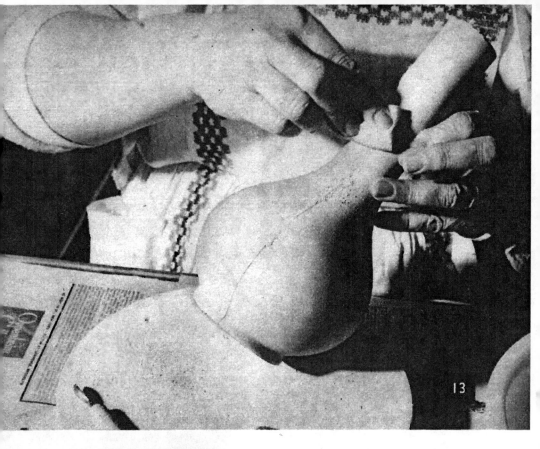

When completely dry, a matter of days, begin the finishing. Use composition sponge or a fettling knife to smooth it off, obliterate imperfections.

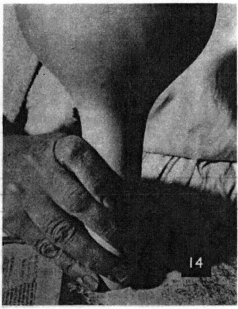

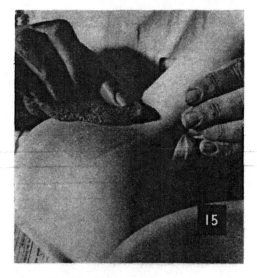

To smooth down the neck of vase, use a piece of grit cloth nailed down on a plywood board. This is done to keep the top of neck even and level.

Next, take soft sponge, immerse it in container of water. Squeeze it out and go over outside of piece with the moist sponge for "finished" look.

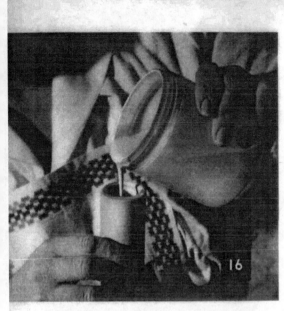

If greenware is to be used to hold water it is necessary to glaze the inside. This is done by slowly pouring glaze into the neck of the vase.

Below, after pouring glaze into vase, wait a few seconds and pour it out slowly while you rotate the vase so that all inside surfaces are covered.

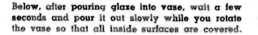

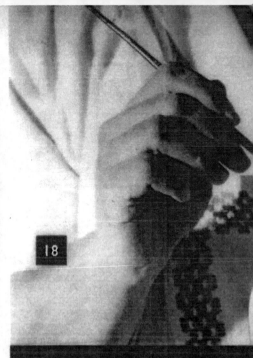

If you've dribbled any glaze on outside, wipe i off with damp sponge. Next, decorate. Usually a underglaze color is used for floral decoration be cause of many colors. For just one or two color use a colored glaze and save the extra step Apply with a soft sable brush and create freely

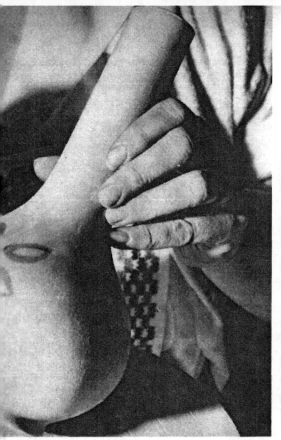

Before placing in kiln see that it's fully dry. If bottom isn't to be glazed, dry-foot the vase: remove all traces of glaze from part that rests on the shelf. If bottom is to be glazed, stilt it to prevent it from sticking to shelf in the kiln.

When decoration is completed you must glaze vase on the outside. One thick coat usually is enough. Flow it on the surface rather than brush it on.

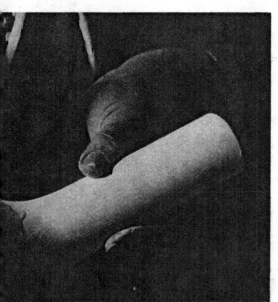

Place ware in kiln, making sure it will clear the door so it won't get crushed. Check the shelves for glaze that may have fallen during previous firing; chip off glaze, kiln-wash any bare spot.

how to throw and decorate a vase

IT IS the inventiveness you display in using the techniques of ceramics that will determine how personal and unusual your pieces will turn out. So experiment!

Here is an example of how you can put your interesting ideas to work. In this instance we start with the throwing of a small-necked vase. When throwing is completed there are many ways of combining techniques to decorate. Here we show how black underglaze engobes are worked into etched lines of varying widths and partially removed to show the black lines on a background of the clay body. Glossy glazes, matte glazes, texture glazes and flowing glazes could be used as well for final decoration. •

Above. Harold Castor first affixes small mound of clay to wheel. With hands wet, he places both thumbs inside center of clay and, by keeping his other fingers outside, shapes and centers clay.

Top right, with right-hand thumb over edge of lip the four fingers and left hand control thickness.

Right, after pulling cylinder to desired height for small-necked vase, cylinder is trimmed off about an inch or two above the finished height.

Below, belly or bowl of vase is formed by pulling areas closer together. Place hands together in cupping shape and, using a pulling movement, bring upper one-third of the cylinder up and in.

Bottom right, small amount of clay left at top is pulled outward and over thumb to form neck and lip. When vase has dried leather-hard, foot is formed. The vase is then allowed to dry slowly.

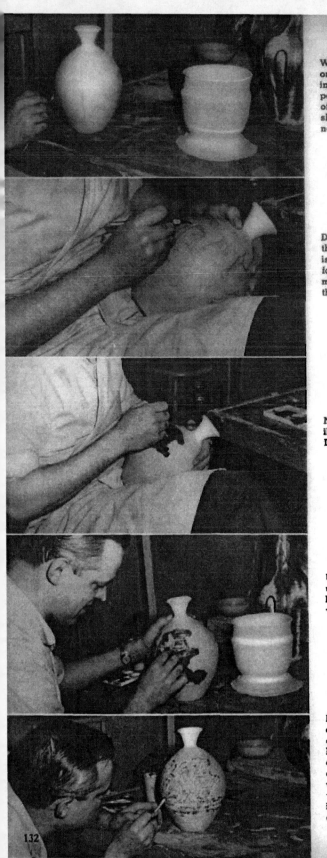

With vase bone-dry, we're ready to decorate and design. Divide up vase area into interesting spaces, using a soft pencil. Then design within the marked-off spaces, keeping harmony with basic shape of vase and working for imaginative rather than realistic patterns.

Design completed, scratching tool (in this case an X-acto Ceramic tool kit) is used to scratch decoration into surface. Vary the lines or they will seem monotonous, and do not scratch deeper than 1/64 to 1/32 inch. Don't "trace."

Now a black underglaze color is heavily brushed over the whole design area. Let it dry; this takes nearly 15 minutes.

Using metal scraper, scrape off area of underglaze color. This will leave the black underglaze within the lines that were scratched, and thus accent them.

If more lines are needed, repeat process until you have a complete design around the vase. Vase is then fired in bisque kiln to 1800° F. After it has cooled from firing, use a transparent glossy glaze for interior in the stoneware temperatures. Spray the exterior with transparent matte glaze and fire it again in kiln to Cone 4. Underglaze color will permeate for diffused effect.

charcoal bag:
new method of copying

Left, charcoal bag is patted onto design of stylized face shown on next page. Above is finished flower bouquet plate made in same way. Use underglaze if bisque or greenware; overglaze for china blank.

HERE IS a wonderfully practical way to use designs and pictures of all types from magazines, newspapers and catalogs. You can save yourself actually many dollars by doing away with stencils, and you will have finished products that are hand-painted.

With a little bit of practice you will be amazed at the beautiful results that can be obtained.

Terese Gluck, who uses this method in her Terri Studio on many thousands of pieces each year, shows how this is done in the photographs on the next two pages.

Materials you will need are a straight pin, the picture you wish to copy, and a small material mesh bag open enough to contain a sufficient amount of powdered charcoal. The mesh has to allow the powdered charcoal to pass through the bag when you pat or dust it on the picture. You can buy powdered charcoal at any art supply store.

First, take your picture and puncture it with the pin all around the outline, making small holes. If there are any eyes or other marks in center areas that you will need to guide you, puncture them as well.

Now, turn the page and see how the process is carried through. •

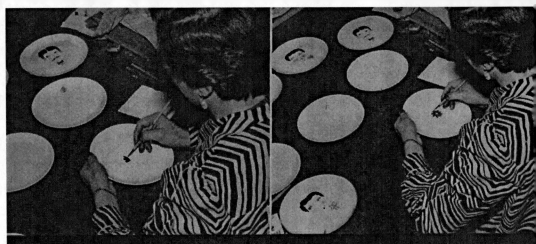

Starting with plate that's been through charcoal bag process (see below) blue cornflower is made. Brush one complete stroke for each side of petal.

Leaning to side for each complete downward petal stroke gives best result. Continue around flower to outline it, leaving small white middle space.

Stylized face design is completed here. If you wish, add spot of background color or a border.

Lay punctured picture on blank dish or tile and dust powdered charcoal on it; hold picture firm.

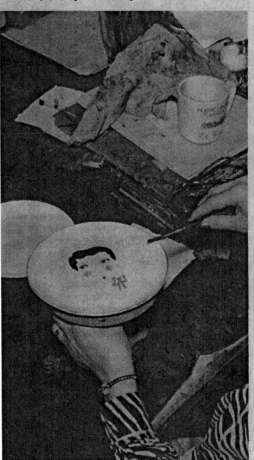

Faint outline of charcoaled figure will serve to guide you. Charcoal will fire away in the kiln.

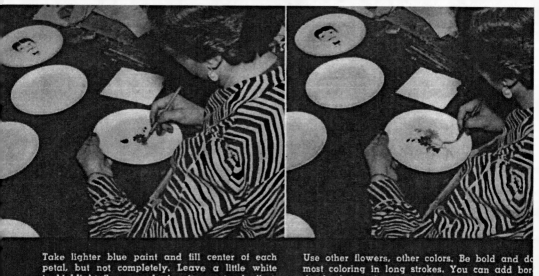

Take lighter blue paint and fill center of each petal, but not completely. Leave a little white to highlight flower and give it a natural effect.

Use other flowers, other colors. Be bold and do most coloring in long strokes. You can add border, background, presentation names or even date.

Use regular sable brush and paint liquid enough to flow easy without running; start on outline.

Black dots for center of eyes is done, and hair is being completed on one of two different faces.

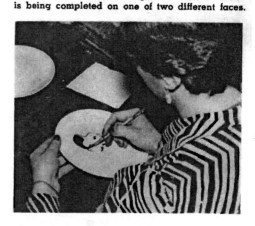

Here, the little bowtie is filled in with contrasting color. Avoid over-literal or fussy touches.

To make the final effect more realistic, you can smudge the paint slightly with the tip of finger.

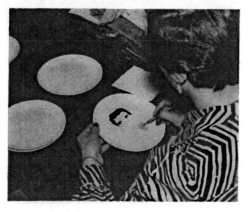

wall and table-top tile

Wall, table and tray are the most obvious places of display for this large and exciting tile. An expert demonstrates how you can make one.

ANOTHER project by Harold Castor of the Sculptors and Ceramic Workshop, this large ceramic tile embodies a design technique that is at an all-time high now in popularity. The steps in making this are clearly shown in the photographs.

Uses for such a tile? There are as many as your imagination can conceive. The tile can be hung on the wall, used to make a tray, be placed on a coffee or end table, etc. However it is used, it can add beauty to your home. This ceramipicture or plaque will be a decorative focal point for your decor. •

Work on large, flat surface or board that's been varnished to protect it, and dust the board with flint to prevent clay from sticking to it. Use a de-aired clay available from clay manufacturers.

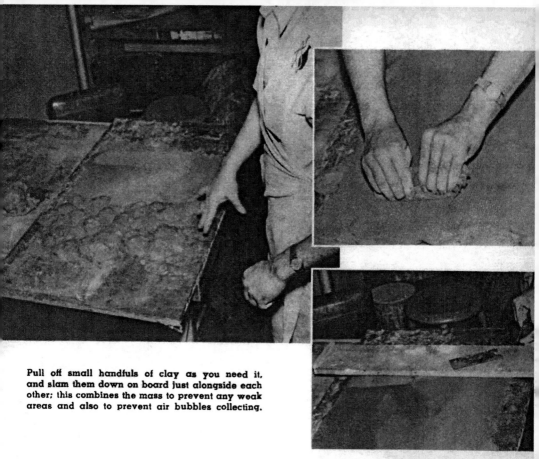

Pull off small handfuls of clay as you need it, and slam them down on board just alongside each other; this combines the mass to prevent any weak areas and also to prevent air bubbles collecting.

Top right, clay is leveled to approximately ¾ inch thick, using a saw-toothed scraper. Scraper provides a textured surface in clay which can be effectively incorporated into the over-all design.

Trim the sides of the clay mass to make an even rectangle. You will find that rectangular shape is more effective in working out design than any form. However, you can vary shape if you so wish.

Plan design and layout on paper and then trace on surface of clay. Mr. Castor prefers to work spontaneously since clay can easily be scraped to hide undesirable lines. Tool has a simple curve.

A wood-wire tool with a straight cutting edge is used to incise and spread clay areas, as well as to develop intriguing planes and variations of dimension and plane. Don't use cramped strokes.

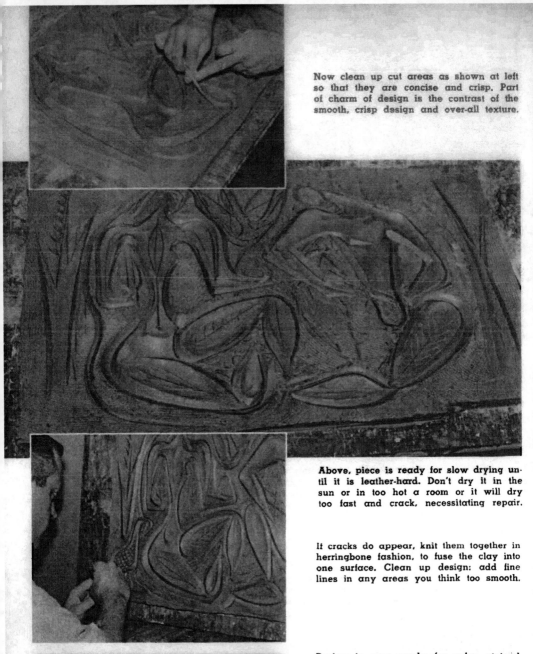

Now clean up cut areas as shown at left so that they are concise and crisp. Part of charm of design is the contrast of the smooth, crisp design and over-all texture.

Above, piece is ready for slow drying until it is leather-hard. Don't dry it in the sun or in too hot a room or it will dry too fast and crack, necessitating repair.

If cracks do appear, knit them together in herringbone fashion, to fuse the clay into one surface. Clean up design; add fine lines in any areas you think too smooth.

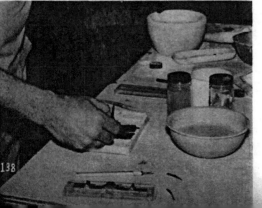

Design is now ready for color—stained engobes in this case. Make engobes with a good powdered underglaze color; raw oxides may be used instead. Recipe used here is (proportion of parts): china clay 25; ball clay 20; ground flint 30; potassium feldspar 17; whiting 2; magnesium carbonate 6. This provides engobe that will fuse to a Jordan clay body in stoneware temperatures. It is white in color, may be stained with underglaze colors. Separate batch into quantities needed for each color. Add water to powdered color, grind it up well.

To apply the engobes to clay use a mottler (wide soft-hair brush) for larger areas, a No. 6 sable brush for smaller areas. Apply color with a dry-brush technique to the background areas first.

Other colors are added to the design. Decide on basic color plan in advance. You may choose all different colors, or work with variation of many blues or reds or greens, depending on tile's use.

Scratch or sgraffito lines in parts of the design right through engobes, to reveal clay underneath and enhance design. When fully dry, place tile in kiln for firing. Be sure glaze from former pieces fired in kiln has been cleaned off: use kiln-wash.

liquid mask
for decorating

Handsome designing in ceramics is easier and more exciting when you use liquid mask to define areas.

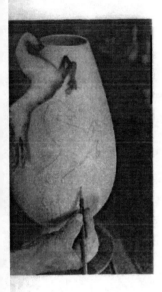

Left, basic pattern of horse is traced on piece of greenware with pencil. Charcoal bag method can be used (page 133), and charcoal marks will fire out in the kiln. Marie Horne is artist on this job.

Use a sable brush and liquid masking material to fill in figure of horse. Let the liquid mask dry for several minutes.

At top right, background was applied—use spray, brush or sponge—with Mayco one-stroke ceramic color. Mask is now peeled off, leaving clean, contrasting surface. If you have difficulty starting mask to peel, lift one corner with a pin.

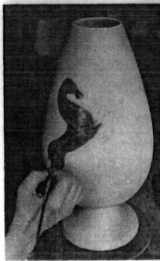

Below left, you can further develop your design by outlining and decorating with brush. Plumes for the head can be made with simple brush stroke; use extra color lines to accent and highlight. Center, use sgraffito tool to reveal white clay body by cutting through ceramic color; this gives a fine effect for horse's tail and mane. Brush or spray glaze over entire decorated surface and then fire it.

glossary
of ceramic terms

ARABIC—A gum used with paint and glaze as a binder.

ARMATURE—A wire-skeleton shape used to build figures on.

BAFFLE—A device used to protect the ware in the kiln.

BALL CLAY—A plastic clay used in the manufacture of stoneware, pottery and chinaware.

BALL MILL—A jar filled with porcelain pebbles that is rotated in order to grind glazes and colors.

BAT—A flat form of plaster on which ceramic pieces are dried.

BENTONITE—Material that is used as an agent to make clay plastic. It is also used as a suspension agent for glazes.

BISCUIT—An unglazed piece of clay that has been fired.

BISQUE—Clay ware that has been fired in the kiln without glaze.

BLANK—Either bisque or greenware undecorated.

BONE CHINA—A believed-to-be stronger porcelain made without feldspar and using bone ash instead.

BLUNGER—A machine with an agitator that is used to churn clay into slip.

BODY—The actual composition of a clay.

CALCINED—A term used in referring to oxides and clays that are fired in a kiln.

CARBONATES—Used to color slip and glazes.

CASTING—Pouring slip into molds and making greenware.

CERAMICS—The art of using clay or earth bodies and firing them into various permanent forms.

CHAMFER—To remove the sharp edges from a mold in order to reduce chipping.

CHINA—Once used to describe a particular ware from the country of its origin (China), but now in general use to describe dinnerware.

CONE—A three-sided pyramidal form of clay and chemicals made to bend at a specific temperature.

CRACKLE—An intentional effect that is given to ware to heighten its age or give a particular design of cracks and lines.

CRAWLING—A glaze defect in which lumps appear.

CRAZE—A split in ware due to imperfect joining of clay and glaze.

glossary

–continued

DECAL—A printed design that can be transferred to ceramics.

DEFLOCCULATE—An additive to slip that prepares it for casting.

DRAWING—Taking fired ware from the kiln.

DRY-FOOT—Leaving the base of any item unglazed.

EARTHENWARE—A porous pottery that is opaque and has been low-fired.

ELECTROLYTES—Chemicals (soda ash and silicate of soda) used to make slip more fluid for casting.

EMBOSSING—Decorating jewelery and pottery with raised designs.

ENGOBE—A slip or liquid clay used for decorating.

FELDSPAR—Fusible rock that can be added to clay.

FETTLE—The process of removing all mold marks from greenware.

FIRING—Applying heat to ware.

FIT—Usually refers to the relation or affinity of the glaze and the clay body. In firing all bodies shrink so it is necessary to use materials that will shrink together. If the glaze and clay body shrink in different proportions they will crack.

FLINT—A silica-quartz.

FLOCCULATE—To make clay plastic by the addition of an acid.

FLUX—An ingredient such as lead, lime or borax used to glaze at a given temperature.

FOOT—Base of any ceramic item.

FRIABLE—That which will crumble easily.

FRIT—Glass that is finely ground and used as a glaze ingredient.

FRITTING—Firing ingredients to a high temperature.

GLAZE—A definite substance of glasslike composition.

GLOST—An English way of saying glaze.

GREENWARE—Clay that is as yet unfired.

GROG—Small particles of sand, bisque or quartz that are added to a clay body to give it strength.

GROUT—Filling the cracks of adjoining tiles with cement.

JIGGER—A partly or wholly automatic device that looks like a potter's wheel and is used to make plates by lowering an outline device onto the back of a revolving mold.

JOLLY—Like a Jigger but used in the production of cups.

KAOLIN—A clay.

KILN—The ovenlike device in which ceramics are fired.

KILN WASH—A solution that is used to cover shelves and the inside of the kiln to prevent the sticking of the ware to the surface supporting it.

LEATHER-HARD—Clay that is hard enough to hold its shape but damp enough to do certain types of work with.

MAJOLICA—Earthenware decorated with a tin-base opaque enamel glaze.

MATTE GLAZE—A glaze having an egg-shell texture.

MENDING SLIP—Slip to which several drops of vinegar have been added.

MODEL—The original creation from which a mold is made.

MOLD—A negative shape of the model which when cast with slip will make a hollow positive.

NATCH—A word to describe the key that lines up the mold parts.

OVERGLAZE—A very low-melting-point glaze that is used to cover a harder glaze.

OXIDES—Used to color glazes and slips.

PEELING—Where the glaze peels off the clay body.

PLAQUE—A form used to hold cones in place in the kiln.

PLASTELINE—A prepared clay made of lanolin, glycerine and clay used extensively for modeling since it doesn't shrink or harden.

PLASTER OF PARIS—A form of gypsum used for making molds and bats.

PORCELAIN—A highly fired, fine, white translucent ceramic ware.

POTTERY—A porous earthenware that may be glazed or not.

PUG MILL—Machine for kneading clay in order to remove air pockets.

PYROMETER—Heat-measuring meter installed in conjunction with a kiln.

REFRACTORY—Nonfusible material capable of resisting high temperature.

SADDLE—A bar of triangular shape used to support shelves and ware in kiln.

SAGGER—A refractory box made of clay and used to protect ware from flames.

SGRAFFITO—A method of decoration in which lines are scratched in slip to reveal undercolors.

SILICATE—A mineral found in flint, quartz and sand.

SIZING—A solution made of soap to prevent plaster from sticking to plaster.

SLIP—Clay in liquid form.

SPARE—A funnel-shaped opening through which slip can enter the mold during the casting process.

SPIT—A piece of the kiln roof or shelf that falls down during firing.

SPUR—A pointed support used to hold up ware during firing.

SPY-HOLE—An opening in the kiln that is used to let out moisture and as a check on how the cone is doing.

STILT—A three-pronged support.

STILT-MARKS—Impressions on ware left when the stilt is removed.

STONEWARE—An opaque, flinty ware that when fired will hold water even if it is not glazed.

TEMPLET—A pattern used in forming ware.

TERRA COTTA—A term usually applied to sculpture that is unglazed.

THIMBLE—A plate support used during firing.

THROWING—Making a form or shape on the potter's wheel

TIN OXIDE—Usually added to glaze to give opacity.

TRAGACANTH—Gum which is used as a binder in pottery.

TURNING—Reforming or trimming work that has been thrown on a wheel.

UNDERGLAZE—Metallic oxides used in painting clay.

VITREOUS—Glasslike.

WATER-OUT—When the kiln is left open while it is on low heat giving the ware-to-be-fired a chance to give off its last moisture.

WEDGING—Pounding clay and cutting it to remove air bubbles.

WHEEL—A wheel used to create forms of pottery, either foot- or power-driven.

manufacturers of ceramic supplies

Kilns
L & L Manufacturing Company, Chester, Pa.
Skutt & Son, P.O. Box 202, Olympia, Wash.
D.H.C. Kiln Co., Box 1762, Fort Worth, Tex.
J.J. Cress Co., P.O. Box 67, Collingswood, N.J.
Paragon Industries, Inc., P.O. Box 4654, Dallas 6, Tex.
Dickinson Pottery Equipment Co., 2424 Glover Pl., Los Angeles, Calif
Harrop Ceramic Service Co., 35 East Gay St., Columbus 15, Ohio
Pereny Equipment Company, 893 Chambers Rd., Columbus 12, Ohio
Richard C. Remmey Son Co., Philadelphia 37, Pa.
Amaco, 4717 W. 16th St., Indianapolis 24, Ind.

Glazes, Paints, Stains
Frieda L. Peterson's, 627 Romero Canyon Rd., Santa Barbara, Calif.
Duncan's Ceramic Products, 4030 N. Blackstone Ave., Fresno, Calif.
Re-Ward, 1985 Firestone Blvd., Los Angeles 1, Calif.
Gare Ceramic Supply Co., 235 Washington St., Haverhill, Mass
Byrne Ceramic Supply Co., Box 96, Ledgewood, N.J.
Specialized Ceramics, 200 West Third St., Plainfield, N.J.
Zirco, 111 N. Western Ave., Los Angeles 4, Calif.
Mayco, 10645 Chandler Blvd., P.O. Box 224, N. Hollywood, Calif.
Ceramichrome, 2111 W. Slauson, Los Angeles 47, Calif.
Francess Art Products, 1651 W. Woodlawn Ave., San Antonio 1, Tex.
Hollywood Ceramic Studio, 6063 N.E. Glisan St., Portland 13, Ore.
Ceramic Color & Chemical Mfg., New Brighton, Pa.
L.H. Butcher, Olympic Blvd., Los Angeles, Calif.
Croxall Chemical & Supply Co., East Liverpool, Ohio
B.F. Drakenfeld & Co., Inc., 45 Park Pl., New York 7, N.Y.
The O. Hommel Co., P.O. Box 475, Pittsburgh 30, Pa
Metal & Thermit Corp., 100 E. 42nd St., New York 17, N.Y.
Tam Products, 111 Broadway, New York, N.Y.
Vitro Manufacturing Co., 60 Greenway Dr., Pittsburgh 4, Pa.
Amaco, 4717 W. 16th St., Indianapolis 24, Ind.

Ceramic Decorators (Lace Tools)
Ace Products Co., P.O. Box 784, Toledo 1, Ohio
Kemper Manufacturing Co., P.O. Box 545, Chino, Calif.

Brushes
Bergan Brush Supplies, 110 Stuyvesant Ave., Lyndhurst, N.J.
Delta Brush Mfg. Corp., 119 Bleecker St., New York, N.Y.
Marx Brush Manufacturing Co., 623 W. 129th St., New York, N.Y.
M. Grumbacher, Inc., 460 W. 34th St., New York, N.Y.

manufacturers –continued

Airbrushes
Paasche Airbrush Co., 1919 Diversey Pkwy., Chicago 14, Ill.

Molds (Press, Pour and Drape)
Inca, 4959 Hollywood Blvd., Hollywood, Calif.
Ludwig Schmid, 838 Genesee St., Trenton 10, N.J.
Atwater Ceramic Molds, 3077 Silver Lake Blvd., Los Angeles 39, Calif.
Lehrhaupt's, 1000 Wilapecko Dr., P.O. Box 345, Asbury Park, N.J.
Zelbur Ceramic Supplies, 1000 Upper Sommerset, Watchung, N.J.
Anne Ank, 11428 S.E. 108th at Court, Renton, Wash.
Charles N. Coulton, 342 Stockman Ave., Morrisville, Pa.
Charles Houston, 3018 West Bullard, Fresno, Calif.
Schenectady Fine Arts, 404 Ballston Rd., Scotia 2, N.Y.
Swoboda's Press Molds, Box 35, Reseda, Calif.

Tiles (Bisque)
Soriano Ceramics, Long Island City 5, N.Y.

Potters Wheels
Craftools, Inc., 401 Broadway, New York 13, N.Y.
American Art Clay Company, 4717 W. 16th St., Indianapolis 24, Ind.
Master Mechanic Manufacturing Co., Burlington, Wisc.

Decals
Stewart's, 12125 Lakewood Blvd., Downey, Calif.

Scales
Toledo Scale Company, 1045 Telegraph Rd., Toledo 1, Ohio
American Art Clay Company, 4717 W. 16th St., Indianapolis 24, Ind.
Craftools, Inc., 401 Broadway, New York 13, N.Y.

Screening Sieves
W.S. Tyler Company, 3614 Superior Ave., Cleveland 14, Ohio
American Art Clay Co., 4717 W. 16th St., Indianapolis 24, Ind.
Craftools, Inc., 401 Broadway, New York 13, N.Y.

Slips and Clay
American Art Clay Co., 4717 W. 16th St., Indianapolis 24, Ind.
Drakenfeld & Co., 45 Park Pl., New York 7, N.Y.
Western Ceramic Supply, 1601 Howard St., San Francisco, Calif.
Jack D. Wolfe Co., 62 Horatio St., New York, N.Y.
Stewart Clay Co., Inc., 137 Mulberry St., New York 13, N.Y.

Slip Mixers
Mixing Equipment Co., 183 Mount Read Blvd., Rochester 11, N.Y.
Patterson Foundry & Machine Co., E. Liverpool, Ohio

Dust Collectors and Shop Vacuums
Craftools, Inc., 401 Broadway, New York 13, N.Y.

Pyrometric Cones and Cone Molds
Edward Orten, Jr., 1445 Summit St., Columbus 1, Ohio

Kiln Furniture
The Louthan Manufacturing Co., E. Liverpool, Ohio
New Castle Refractories Co., New Castle, Pa.
Potters Supply Co., East Liverpool, Ohio
Shenango Refractories, P.O. Box 120, New Castle, Pa.

Spraying Equipment
Craftools, Inc., 401 Broadway, New York 13, N.Y.
American Art Clay Company, 4717 W. 16th St., Indianapolis 24, Ind.

Ball Mills and Accessories
Craftools, Inc., 401 Broadway, New York 13, N.Y.

Clay and Plaster Tools
Craftools, Inc., 401 Broadway, New York 13, N.Y.
American Art Clay Company, 4717 W. 16th St., Indianapolis 24, Ind.

Wedging Boards, Plaster Bats, Cabinets, etc.
American Art Clay Company, 4717 W. 16th St., Indianapolis 24, Ind.
Craftools, Inc., 401 Broadway, New York 13, N.Y.

Modeling and Sculpture Tools
Craftools, Inc., 401 Broadway, New York 13, N.Y.
American Art Clay Company, 4717 W. 16th St., Indianapolis 24, Ind.
Stewart Clay Co., Inc., 137 Mulberry St., New York 13, N.Y.
Drakenfeld & Co., 45-47 Park Pl., New York 7, N.Y.
X-Acto, Inc., 48-67 Van Dam St., Long Island City 1, N.Y.

CPSIA information can be obtained at www.ICGtesting.com
Printed in the USA
BVOW04s2348080914

366033BV00015B/169/P